This was supposed to be about something else. It's not what we expected it to be. But once we started, it took on a life of its own. And now it's this. And as a result it's hopefully better than the original idea.

Such is life. Such happy things only happen if you **get started** on something. There's something to say about this on page 131.

Originally the book was intended specifically for people teetering on the brink of setting up their own first business and in need of a friendly shove in the right direction. But it changed.

The impetus needed to start a business is the same as anyone teetering on the brink of *anything*. So for you – this is your kick in the pants.

If you want to do something but secretly fear you're never going to do it, whatever that might be, then this might help you:

- Go to the Amazon
- Throw yourself into retraining
- Lose a dress size
- Go back to school
- Write a book
- Ditch your partner
- Take your company in a ne
- Create art
- Learn to play polo
- Seek the promotion you want
- ...OR set up your own business.

As a result it's not written just for the entrepreneurial business person but for the entrepreneurial in spirit. The lessons, the advice, the nagging, the cartoons, the jokes, the exaggerations and the things that possibly never really happened... all these things apply to anyone trying to cross that bridge between their dreams and their reality.

Talking of the things-that-probably-never-really-happened...

A Tibetan Lama was speaking to a group of monks and to make a point, pulled out a large jar, set it on the table in front of him, produced a few fist-sized rocks, and placed them, one by one, into the jar.

When no more rocks would fit inside, he asked: "Is this jar full?" Everyone said: "Yes." He reached under the table and pulled out a bucket of gravel, dumped some in and shook the jar, the gravel worked between the rocks. Again, he asked: "Is this jar full?" The monks were catching on. "Probably not," one answered.

"Good!" he replied and reached under the table and brought out a bucket of sand. He dumped the sand into the jar until it filled all the crevices. Once more he asked: "Is this jar full?"

"No!" the monks shouted. "Good!" he said and grabbed a pitcher of water and poured it until the jar was filled to the brim. Then he asked, "What is the point of this illustration?" One young monk responded, "The point is, no matter how full your day you can always fit some more things in."

"No," the speaker replied, "the point is that if you don't put the big rocks in first, you'll never get them in at all. What are the priorities in your life?"[1]

The **FIRST**
reason to start
something now...

YOU CAN

You might have an itch.

Life is short.

If you've got something you want to do...
now is a good time to start.

Here are four reasons why...

"Only put off until tomorrow what you are willing to die having left undone."

Pablo Picasso

- What then, after a few weeks sitting on a beach, would you like to be getting on with?

- Do you want to write a book, start a band, study, renovate your house, leave your partner, your job, the town you live in and travel far and wide?

- What's it going to be? What do you want to do? Get a pen and paper and write it down. Now.

- Write down the things you'd do and the things, people and places it would involve. If it involves more money than you currently have, you're granted a limitless fund for anything you want to do.

- The money is there so that there's no financial barrier to you doing what you've often talked about.

- Find an image from a magazine (or download one from online and print off), something that depicts what it is you really want to do.

Take a couple of years out

Supposing you could take the next 2 years off from your normal life? You didn't have to worry about where you live, earning a living, paying the bills, what family, friends and colleagues would think of what you do in those next 24 months.

Now, what are you going to do in this time? Shop, surf the web and update your status? Maybe you'll spend your time sitting on a beach talking about what you're going to do over the next few months? Or will you be itching to get on with what you've been thinking about and talking about?

The speed of life

This book is about starting.

It's about shifting from the static to the active state; the state where things happen because you initiated them.

It's about shifting gears, moving direction, transforming what you do with your day, your week, your time and taking control; it's about deliberately putting one foot in front of the other and moving with purpose instead of being carried along by the current.

There's never been a better time to start something. Now more than ever we live in a world of opportunity.

But the downside to this world of opportunity – brought about by new technology and new social and working conventions – is a world that seduces us into drifting through life.

Things like: shopping, web-surfing, casual tweeting, photo-commenting and status-updating. It's not that these things aren't fun or even good. But while it might feel like you're "doing" – in large part thanks to the power of billions of dollars of marketing – you might have a feeling that there's got to be more to life.

Life has a sting in the tail.

It's shorter than we expect.

And it races by while we're working out what's really important and what actually isn't.

As time roars past our ears we drift, deliberate, doubt and take ourselves too seriously yet all the while we talk about what we would, could and should do to make it better.

And then it's gone.

So let's walk the talk.

Because there's never been a better time, or a more urgent time, to start doing the things you want to do.

Let's dance.

"What is past is prologue."

William Shakespeare

"Eyes front!"

Any drill sergeant in any
army anywhere

PART 1

TICK TOCK

"Courage is being scared to death...
and saddling up anyway."

John Wayne

"Oh, the places you'll go!"

Dr. Seuss

Marshmallows

...to Doing

How to Get From
Talking...

Leave regret

The Discomfort zone

Flush   Seize control

Embrace fear   **3**   If only...

**FEAR AND
REGRET**

The speed of life

1 **TICK TOCK**

Would, could, should...

Catch up   Shifting gears

If not now,
then...never?

Stop daydreaming?

2 **THE ITCH**

What do you want?

What makes you happy?   Know yourself

Where are you scratching?

"Viva gumption!"

STOP TALKING, START DOING
ACTION BOOK

Practical Tools and Exercises to Give
You A Kick in the Pants

Sháá Wasmund, MBE

CAPSTONE
A Wiley Brand

The wheels are greased.

Our connected world makes it possible for people to actualize dreams, ideas and initiative in ways our forebears could not even dream of.

1.
Whatever you want to know is accessible instantly.

Want to collect fountain pens from around the world, want to learn how to collect truffles, want to find someone to build a mobile phone app for you in another continent, want to retrain, want to research how to bicycle across the world...? No problem. It's all at your fingertips.

Try it now.

Put a couple of these into a search engine and see what comes up.

How to collect fountain pens from around the world

How to collect truffles

Mobile phone app builders in India and China

How to cycle across the world.

2.

Need to locate expert help?

Then connect with people who can help you. The soaring development of the social web has demolished barriers between you and the expertise you need. It empowers you to ask friends of friends (and friends of friends of friends) if they can offer advice, make introductions, share experiences.

Try it now.

Who do you know who's already doing or has done what you want to do? Get in touch with them. Ask to meet them, talk on the phone or email them and find out how they did it. What are their top tips?

3. Tribe up.

Whatever it is you want to start doing – a business, a work of art, a social project, setting up a partnership of website information architects – there are people somewhere in the world who share your passion. Want to find people to trade antique fountain pens with? There are thousands of them. It doesn't take Sherlock Holmes to find people who share your passion. You can support each other, learn from each other, do business with each other. The author Seth Godin[2] calls these groups of shared passions: "Tribes."

Try it now.

Here's a few ideas to find your tribe:

Meetup (www.meetup.com) – an online networking site that facilitates offline group meetings in various localities around the world. You can find and join groups unified by a common interest.

Facebook groups – these provide a dedicated space for people to communicate their shared interests, so a great way to find and connect with like-minded sets of people.

Peoplehunt – an app which connects individuals with reciprocal interests. For example, you can find someone to practise another language with, or give you guidance about online marketing.

4.
The "barriers to entry" have collapsed.

OK, so that's a business term and we're not just talking about business. But the point is that the cost of setting up many businesses or even non-business projects has collapsed. Most digital start-ups don't even need an office but work from shared space or coffee shops. This has, for example, had an impact on the venture capital world. The power used to be in the hands of the VCs because you needed money to set up a business and they would exact a heavy price for the cash. Now that it doesn't cost so much to start up, the power is with people who have ideas and the "gumption" to make them happen.

Viva la Revolución!

Viva gumption!

5.
You're already at the centre of the universe.

And if in fact you are starting a business or collecting fountain pens from around the world, the global markets are wide open for business. From your front room.

The fat is
in the pan.

Get cooking.

The **SECOND**
reason to start
something now...

**Unconventional is
Conventional**

The boat is being rocked.

The conventions of society that dictated the correct way to behave and whose arched eyebrows used to hold people's dreams in check are vanishing. In the big cities they're already long gone. The world is too connected for that and it moves too fast.

1. Sixty years ago a gentleman wouldn't go to work without a hat on; ten years ago they stopped wearing ties. Now you don't have go into work to go to work... so who knows what people are wearing. But the point is: who cares?!

Society cares less about conformity than it used to. This makes it easier to swim against the current. Easier to do something different, to challenge convention. If you want to give up your job and travel round the world, learn to juggle, join a commune – your neighbours might cough and shake their heads but you can cope with that...Or they might just tell you how they always wanted to do the same thing.

2. The concept of a job for life is long gone. The tramlines that used to confine a career from start to finish; from apprenticeship to grave aren't imposed by anyone but you. It's not unusual to hold down three part-time jobs at once or to shift jobs every couple of years. In response to the absence of job security we have had to become more agile in our approach to work. Self-employment is soaring.

3. You are going to live a long time. Life expectancy goes up and up. If you're going to be around a long time you might as well do something you enjoy for as much of that time as possible.

Pimp your ride.

The boat is *already* being rocked.

Some examples of how lifestyle, work, society and leisure are changing.

The most entrepreneurial country in the West is built on failure

The net number of U.S. startups versus closures is minus 70,000.
(Source: US Census Bureau, Longitudinal Business Database)

Folk managing themselves and themselves alone

There are over 22 million non-employer businesses. Meaning they have no boss and they have no staff underneath them.

They just get up and do.

(Source: US Census Bureau)

Locations where work was conducted during the past month

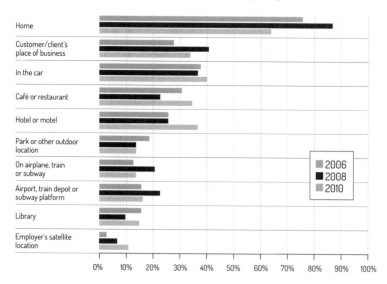

(Source: Telework 2011 by World at Work using data collected by the Dierenger Research Group Inc and World at Work)

Folk escaping the cubicle on a daily basis

3.7 million employees (2.5% of the workforce) now work from home at least half the time.

(Source: Based on an analysis of 2005-2014 American Community Survey (US Census Bureau) data conducted by GlobalWorkplaceAnalytic.com)

Folk escaping the cubicle for a long time

Of the 2014 FORTUNE 100 Best Companies, 72% offer sabbaticals.

(Source: Rohman, Jessica, "How great workplaces support work-life balance", 19 May 2014, www. greatplacetowork.com)

Lots of people share the same starting line

It's estimated that one in every eight workers in the United States has at some point been employed by McDonald's.

(Source: New York Times)

...And lots of people don't: being different is becoming the new norm

In 2013, 12.5% of the UK population was born outside the UK. That's up from 8.6% in 2003.

(Source: The Migration Observatory www.migrationobservatory.ox.ac.uk)

Small businesses are everywhere

There were 5 million micro-businesses (those with less than 10 staff) in the UK in 2014, accounting for 96% of all businesses.

(Source: BIS, Business Population Estimates 2014

You will live longer
So do something you enjoy.

	Male	Female
1930	58.1	61.6
1940	60.8	65.2
1950	65.6	71.1
1960	66.6	73.1
1970	67.1	74.7
1980	70.0	77.4
1990	71.8	78.8
2000	74.3	79.7
2007	75.4	80.4
2010	76.2	81.0

Life expectancy in the United States

(Source: National Center for Health Statistics, National Vital Statistics Reports, vol. 54, no. 19, June 28, 2006 and Vol. 63, No. 7, November 6, 2014. Web: www.cdc.gov/nchs)

And there's a lot of us around
About 6.5% of all the people who have ever lived are alive today.

(Source: Carl Haub, "How many people have ever lived on Earth?" Population Reference Bureau)

The dominant habitat of the global species is the city

Percentage of population living in cities:

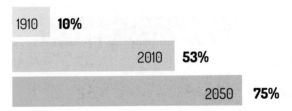

(Source: London School of Economics and Deutsche Bank's Alfred Herrhausen Society: The Endless City)

And yet people want to escape the concrete habitat and farm their own food...(but sometimes they have to wait)

The average time on a waiting list for an allotment in Britain: 3 years. In parts of London the wait is 10 years.

According to one survey, the London Borough of Camden has a waiting list of 40 years.

(Source: Survey by LV Insurance 2009 quoted in "Allotment waiting lists: a barometer of our times," David Derbyshire, February 15th, 2011. http://allotmentblog.dailymail.co.uk)

Power is shifting East

At the end of 2004, there were 6,704 buildings over 11 stories built since 1990. In 2011, that grew to over 20,000 buildings.

(Source: https://en.wikipedia.org/wiki/List_of_tallest_buildings_in_Shanghai)

You've no excuse not to find your tribe!

Take MeetUp, for example. This online network of social groups makes it easy for people to connect with others who share the same interests. They meet online and offline.

Number of meetings per month: 570,895
Number of monthly RSVPs: 3.93 million
Countries holding meet ups: 180

(Source: Meetup, 2015)

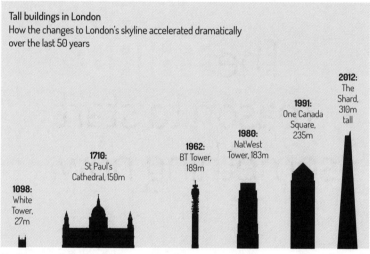

Tall buildings in London
How the changes to London's skyline accelerated dramatically over the last 50 years

1098:
White Tower, 27m

1710:
St Paul's Cathedral, 150m

1962:
BT Tower, 189m

1980:
NatWest Tower, 183m

1991:
One Canada Square, 235m

2012:
The Shard, 310m tall

(Source: Data obtained from http://en.wikipedia.org/wiki/List_of_tallest_buildings_and_structures_in_London)

You're not who you were

It takes seven to ten years for the human body to renew every single cell. Your body is younger than you are. Whose issues are holding you back?!

Catch up

The **THIRD**
reason to start
something now...

**The Feeling
of Emptiness**

Is that all there is?

Indeed. Technology has brought the world to our fingertips and helped knock down the prison walls of convention but at the same time it also threatens to suck the meaning out of life. The antidote is to take the initiative; to start something yourself; something that has purpose. Here are some examples of the areas to watch out for:

1. **The shop floor.** The meaningless grind of the factory production line has now seeped into the world of the white collar worker. As factory jobs moved from the West to the East the economies of the West have become dominated by so-called "knowledge workers". The component parts of these jobs have been fragmented just like assembly line work and have had the satisfaction sucked out in just the same way. Rules and manuals govern every decision and reserve initiative and decision-making for the computer and the head office. You become emotionally disconnected from your job...You get an itch.

2. **Long days.** The working day gets longer and longer. The macho pride in the length of the hours you work, in the end, means...what? You have less free time. So what are you going to DO with it?

3. **The banks and the financial crisis.** The fruits of their labour, for an awful lot of people, was the ability to maximize their debt and buy the biggest house they could afford in the area they wanted to live. And then the market crashed. And your house price went "sayonara, baby". Which was when you began to think to yourself: Is that all there is? Where's my job satisfaction if it isn't in the mortgage? What would I rather be doing with my free time? With my money? How am I going to change things?

In response to the feeling of emptiness and a search for meaning we are witnessing the emergence of business entities created for reasons other than solely monetary profit. The writer Daniel Pink[3] describes the movement as one of **Purpose Maximizers** – people and entities driven by things other than money:

- The open-source movement has created powerful and valuable businesses and organizations such as Wikipedia (the online encyclopedia), Mozilla Firefox (the web browser and email) and Linux (the operating system used by many large organizations). Such businesses work because thousands of people freely give their time and skills. These are being formalized as "for social-benefit" organizations as opposed to "for profit".

- The US state of Vermont recently created a low profit limited liability corporation. This allowed economic entities to be created whose purpose was to create a modest profit, for sure, but primarily to create a social benefit. Look at it this way, company law generally requires businesses to be created with the purpose of maximizing profits for the benefit of shareholders. Now they can have a different purpose – enshrined in law.

- The Nobel Prize winning economist Muhammad Yunus[4] has created the concept of social businesses. Rather than being "for profit" these are "non-loss" companies. They must be economically self-sustaining but are not created to make a profit for the founders but to provide some form of social good.

It's not that seeking profit is necessarily bad. Far from it. But this trend shows a growing appreciation of how people can be powerfully motivated and compensated by the intrinsic meaning of what they DO and not just by a financial bonus scheme.

Waiting for an urban plot of land to work on before you start waiting to leave the city and grow your own vegetables in your own garden?

Don't confine your dream to waiting.

Get your hands dirty.

Start.

The **FOURTH**
reason to start
something now...

**That Ticking
Sound...**

Tick

One thing technology hasn't changed.

You won't live forever.

You might live a bit longer but that's all the more reason to start pursuing the life you want, not just the one you've ended up with.

Another thing technology hasn't changed: clichés about the passage of time. The thing is, clichés and truisms stick around through the generations for a reason...

And the sands of time are running out even as you turn the page.

 **Let's get moving.**

Tock

106 BILLION LESSONS WHY NOW IS THE RIGHT TIME TO START DOING...

100 billion
...and counting

The number of human beings estimated to have died in the whole history of the universe and everything. Ever.[5]

7.3 billion

The total number of human beings alive today at the most populous time in the history of the whole world ever. *Ever*. So far.

ONE

The total number of chances to live your life that you get in the history of the world, the Universe and all the space time dimensions visited in all the episodes of *Star Trek* including spin-offs ever...before you are added to the 110 billion or so gravestones ever put into the ground by the time you kick the bucket.

Write down your thoughts about why NOW is the right time for you to start doing...

Question: Do you see yourself in this picture?

Inside the ropes, there are two guys fighting for their dreams.

Both dared mighty things and both have had great stories to tell.

And outside the ropes there are a thousand faces watching other people fight for their dreams.

The point?

You don't want to be an anonymous face in the crowd of your own life story.

That's a life of regret.

You gotta face your fears and climb inside the ropes.

PART 2

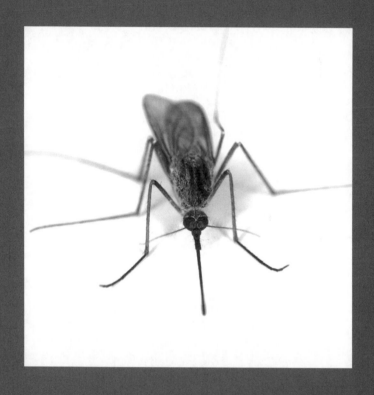

THE ITCH

"One half of knowing what it is you want to do is knowing what you must give up before you get it."

Sidney Howard

"We need to first define the problem. If I had an hour to save the world I would spend 59 minutes defining the problem and one minute finding solutions."

Albert Einstein

You've been stung.

And now you've got an itch.

A mosquito bite-sized itch.

Or an itch the size of Mount Everest, perhaps.

Maybe you will be forever restless until you write that novel, start that business, get that job, or work in that industry.

The first thing is to recognize the itch.

Recognize it and you're halfway there. Because then at least you know which way to focus your attention.

The train

So the first step is to know what you want. What is it you want to start changing?

Is it about introducing something new into your life or is it something bigger?

There is no universal right answer. Just a right answer for you.

So, grab a pen and paper, pull out your iPad or pick up a piece of chalk...

Write down the one thing that you want to do most. The one thing that would make the most difference or bring the biggest happiness into your life.

Keep it simple and focused.

This won't work

This will

Do it now. Let's get this doing muscle working!

Where do you want to sit on the train?

All aboard the: Your Life Express

You can have a happy life choosing a job path that allows you to finish at 5pm, every day on the dot so that you can leave the job in the office and play the odd round of golf on long summer evenings.

But bear in mind that while such a lifestyle might seem like perfection to you, it might smack of claustrophobic routine for someone else.

Their ideal might be found in constant change or, perhaps, manic deadlines (writers have been known to be like that, so it is said).

On a more pragmatic note, it might be that you require a predictable and relatively undemanding job so that you can plough your real energy into another project – a business of your own, or maybe your passion for cooking. Once you recognize the virtues of your job you might find you've got less to be frustrated about.

And then there's the brightly lit, hard-as-concrete realities of your personal situation.

Most people are limited by obligations to family or economic constraints. Others by physical infirmities. These are real and naturally you have to marry your sky-high ambitions with some smart navigation around such obstacles. Your options can be as wide open as the seven seas, if you want them to be – rejoice and make the most of it!

Create your own Life Express

1. Write down all the big events and experiences in your life so far. Think of achievements, successes and happy experiences. Think of difficult, challenging and unhappy experiences too.

- Think about the turning points in your life – starting school college or university. Moving home, making friends and other significant relationships, starting a new job, leaving a job, birth of your children, bereavements. Write down too, any special travel experiences and holidays, celebratory events, parties and festivals.

- Write down any opportunities you didn't take up.

- Write down the year things happened, next to each event and experience.

2. Now take a very large piece of paper, the size of a flip chart piece of paper, (or create a large piece by sticking smaller pieces of paper together) and draw a faint line from one side of the paper to the other.

3. Now write down each experience and event, in order of the year it happened, along the line. Write each experience and event as far above or below the line as you think best represents each experience. For example, if being fired from a job was the most difficult thing that has happened to you it might go far below the line. If the best thing that has happened so far was a period of travel, place that high above the line.

Add symbols, emoticons and pictures to each experience and event.

4. Draw a line to connect all the events – the line will of course, go up and down as it connects all the events across the years.

5. Now look at your "Life Express". Look at how far you've come and how many ups and downs, twists and turns have occurred in your life.

- Which of these events and experiences just happened to you? Which ones were deliberate decisions?

- Times when you've felt most energized and useful?

- What skills and abilities were you using? What environment? Which relationships? What are the common themes? These themes are often a good indication of what's going to work well for you in future.

- If an event was your decision and it turned out well, how did you feel about it then?

- If a decision you made didn't turn out so well, how did you feel then and how do you feel now?

- Despite the ups and downs in your life, you've got this far. Where are you going next? Do you think it will be a straight line?

Hopefully, this exercise will have shown you that there will be events, experiences, good times, difficult times, decisions to be made. They're going to happen anyway. Don't let them stop you. Start doing!

"What a man can be, he must be."

Abraham Maslow

Where are you scratching?

Observe yourself to locate your itch.

Alas, not everyone has an overwhelming urge to do a particular THING. Sometimes there's just a feeling that there might be more to life.

For those who are blessed with a "calling" then it's easy to answer the question: "What's your passion?"

But for a lot of us it's more difficult.

The writer Daniel Pink[6] says this is the wrong question in any event. The right one, he says, is to ask:

"What do you do?"

The answer you should be looking for is not necessarily what you do as a career: I'm an accountant/I'm a full-time mother but it's the other stuff that you do. In other words, Pink urges that you instead monitor yourself to see what it is that you do alongside your headline activity.

By this he means to examine what it is you do in your free time. Where does your mind wander when you have a spare moment? What do you make time for? In your quieter moments at work do you write poetry, doodle, scratch recipes and ingredients on a pad of paper, edit your photographs, check out the latest science on endurance athletes or something else entirely? Where does your mind flow to? What websites and blogs do you gravitate to? What do you do even if you're not being paid to do it?

There's your answer. Or at least one of them.

"In the next 20 years we shall become much richer, but will we really be any richer as people – happier?"

Richard Nixon, 1968, US President

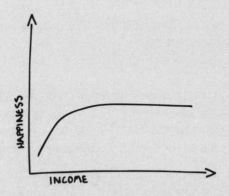

The economist Richard Easterlin argued that once your basic needs are covered, an increase in average income does not necessarily lead to increased levels of average happiness. His analysis showed that although wealth, or income per person, rose steadily between 1947 and 1970, the average happiness reported by individuals did not rise no matter how much more they earned. Some economists have challenged this recently but most accept that the link between income and happiness is not straightforward.

Why are people driven to DO things other than make money?

In a world obsessed by wealth and celebrities (who in turn display and represent wealth) it might strike a wrong note to say money isn't the answer. Those who don't have it certainly know it would make their life easier; and yet those who are wealthy will proclaim earnestly: "money doesn't make you happy".

If money doesn't make you happy what should you be doing?

How do you know whether scratching your itch will make you happy?

The psychologist Abraham Maslow[7] argued that pursuing that which you are passionate about and driven by will make you happy because it fulfils your "highest needs".

A human being is driven by five categories of needs, he said:

Physical, Security, Social, Esteem, and Self-Actualization.

Money will generally help you satisfy some of these needs but not all of them and most probably not the one that is most personal – Self-Actualization.

What you need to HAVE and what you want to DO

Maslow's Hierarchy of Needs

Toward the bottom of the pyramid are your basic needs. You need to deal with these first of all (who cares about your passion to sail the Caribbean if you're too tired to think?).

You need food to eat, you need to be dry and warm. Then you need to be physically safe and you need security (including financial security).

These two lower level needs guarantee survival and are a minimum requirement. Then you need a sense of belonging – whether it's to a family, a group of friends, or for some, a shared passion through some interest group.

With these basic needs satisfied you are then driven, said Maslow to seek comfort from having a good reputation and being held in high regard not just by others but importantly – also by yourself.

And indeed, it's true that a fast car might be a way of gaining high esteem in some people's eyes...but so might doing charity work or being an expert urban beekeeper.

With all these four needs satisfied you can focus on your itch or what Maslow called "Self-Actualization". This is about realizing your full potential. "What a man can be, he must be," Maslow said.

Your strong need may be to be the best teacher you can be, the owner of your own business, a skilled photographer or the person who can hold their breath underwater for the longest time.

Needless to say, the act of Actualization is in the act of doing... not talking about doing.

In defence of talking

Don't get the wrong idea.

This urgency to turn talking into doing doesn't mean talking is bad. On the contrary, talking is good.

It's one of the best ways to explore your ideas and your options and hold them up to examination to see whether your plans make sense and your reasoning is sound.

The thing about talking is that it's a surefire way to know that something is bugging you. If you talk about something a lot then the chances are that it's treading heavily on your psychic radar and that's a sign you need to do something about it. So listen up.

And if you're serious about doing something then it makes every type of sense to talk it through with people.

Talking is one half of one of the most indispensible commodities of life – and that is conversation.

But when you talk about what you're going to do...talk with purpose.

People will listen to you if they believe that when you say you're going to do something you really will walk the talk.

You could call it the Ronseal approach after the famous UK advertising campaign for the no-nonsense DIY brand which:

DOES WHAT IT SAYS ON THE TIN

More inspirationally you might call it the Muhammad Ali approach. He was as spell-binding a speaker as he was a mesmerizing force in the ring.

The Ali lesson: If you talk big and deliver big then you truly are great.

Braggadocio

Brag`ga*do"cio (?), n.

[From Braggadocchio, a boastful character in Spenser's *The Faerie Queene*]

1. A braggart; a boaster; a swaggerer.
Dryden.

2. Empty boasting; mere brag; pretension.

Webster's Revised Unabridged Dictionary (G. & C. Merriam Co., 1913, edited by Noah Porter)

...Or as Mr. T from the A-Team might say:

"Fool, you're wearing my ears out."

Self-belief and big words – if they're not backed up by action – leave people flat. If you're saying the word "I" in every sentence then you need to do something:

...something like pipe down.

Unless...Well, here's someone who talked really big and delivered on it...

I am the astronaut of boxing.
Joe Louis and Dempsey were just jet
pilots. I'm in a world of my own.

I am the greatest, I said that even before I knew I was.

It's hard to be humble, when you're as great as I am.

If you even dream of beating me you'd
better wake up and apologize.

It's the repetition of affirmations that leads
to belief. And once that belief becomes a
deep conviction, things begin to happen.

I figured that if I said it enough, I would convince
the world that I really was the greatest.

It's not bragging if you can back it up.

Muhammad Ali

Heavyweight champion of the world

And perhaps more thoughtfully:

> "A man who views the world the same at fifty as he did at twenty has wasted thirty years of his life."
>
> "He who is not courageous enough to take risks will accomplish nothing in life."
>
> "It isn't the mountains ahead to climb that wear you out; it's the pebble in your shoe."
>
> "Silence is golden when you can't think of a good answer."
>
> Muhammad Ali
> Heavyweight champion of the world

...and listening

(The other half of the indispensable commodity of conversation.) You can't listen if you're too busy talking. And it's a great way to learn. Don't just listen to the top notes either, listen to the background noise too. Often it's the small things that go unnoticed that provide the real clues.

A rhetorical quiz to reinforce the point:
You meet someone smarter than you.

Do you:
a/ shut up and listen
or do you
b/ talk their ears off?

Do you talk more than you listen?

Tick the statements that apply to you.

1. I prefer to talk about things rather than think about them.	
2. I like to listen to information that will help me solve a problem or give me new ideas.	
3. I encourage other people to talk, and I ask appropriate questions.	
4. Sometimes, I get so caught up in what I have to say that I am unaware of how others are reacting.	
5. I can always tell when someone doesn't understand what I'm saying.	
6. When talking with people, I'm often aware of their body language.	
7. I can easily divert or end conversations that don't interest me.	
8. I enjoy initiating and leading a conversation.	
9. When I hear a different point of view I like to review what I've just heard and think about how I want to respond.	
10. If asked, I'm happy to tell other people what I've done and achieved.	

11. I'm not afraid to interrupt someone when they're talking.	
12. I find it easy to explain what I'm thinking or planning.	
13. I like to hear about different possibilities, options and potential ways forward.	
14. I'm good at giving people advice.	
15. I'm happy to join in conversations on topics I don't know much about.	
16. I like to hear information that will help me learn or discover something.	
17. In a group conversation, I like to have time to think before I say what's on my mind.	
18. When describing something, I sometimes exaggerate.	
19. I like to take my time finding out the facts before I say what I think.	
20. I'm interested in finding out what other people feel and think.	

If you ticked question numbers:

1, 4, 7, 8, 10, 11, 12, 14, 15, 18

...give yourself a point for each statement you ticked. Add up the ticks.

If you ticked question numbers:

2, 3, 5, 6, 9, 13, 16, 17, 19, 20

...give yourself a point for each the statement you ticked. Add up the ticks.

If most of the statements you ticked are the first group, you're more of a talker.

If most of the statements you ticked are the second group, you're probably more of a listener.

Talkers

You like to talk! You like to talk in a lively, spontaneous, opportunistic way. You like an audience! You don't hesitate to add your own comments to a discussion or even change the subject. You may have strong opinions and will speak out on what you think is right. You probably enjoy describing all aspects and details of a situation or an idea and talk about what should and could be done.

It's time to Stop Talking. Start Doing!

Listeners

You listen more than you talk and don't like to interrupt.
You'd rather say nothing than say something wrong. You like to "read between the lines" and really understand what's going on. You probably like to hear different points of view and know about different ways of doing things.

Good for you! Just make sure you do something with what you've heard and listened to!

You know the one about the reason you were given TWO ears and ONE mouth...

Two Warnings...

Applause Warning

Examine your reasons carefully. Are you doing it because it's something you want to do or are you seeking it for what it will say about you. Begging applause from a fickle audience is a dangerous way to chase your dreams. You are dependent on other people. This is not Self-Actualization.

On a scale of 1 – 5:
How important is it that what you want to do means that:

1. Other people will agree with or approve of what I want to do ☐

2. I'll make a lot of money ☐

3. There will be awards, medals or trophies to be won ☐

4. I'll be better than others at doing what I want to do ☐

5. Other people will appreciate my efforts ☐

6. I'll be recognized and rewarded for my efforts ☐

Score ☐

The higher your score is over 15, the more you are relying on extrinsic motivators: applause, recognition from others and material rewards.

Responsibility Warning

If this thing you seek will have a significant effect on your life or those of others (particularly your dependants)...think carefully about the reasons why you are doing it before taking the plunge.

On a scale of 1 – 5:
How important is it that what you want to do means that:

1. I'll enjoy what I want to do. I'm interested and fascinated; it will hold my attention ☐

2. I'll learn new skills or knowledge ☐

3. What I do will match my values; what's important to me ☐

4. I'll feel capable, competent and confident ☐

5. I'll be able to make my own decisions ☐

6. I'll work with and cooperate with other people ☐

Score ☐

The higher your score over 15 points, the more you are motivated by intrinsic factors: enjoyment, challenge, feeling good about yourself, a sense of autonomy and being connected to others.

How doing attracts criticism and complaints for all sorts of understandable but wrong-headed reasons...

We all live interdependent lives.

We take comfort from seeing people in the office every day even if we don't talk to them or maybe don't even like them.

Seeing the usual things happen for the usual reasons means there are no nasty surprises. Routine is comfortable.

In a way it's a confirmation that we're doing the right thing...even if part of that routine is to get together around the coffee machine and moan about how awful everything is.

So if you are about to do something different – by turning your intention into action and stepping into the ring – you will be upsetting the status quo and consequently you may find you suddenly create an army of critics.

Um. That's your fault. YOU'RE BEING SCARY.

Because when you change, your relationship with everything and everyone else changes too.

This really does scare people. Those people who are freaked out that you just turned talk into action will probably redouble their criticism of your ideas; they'll try to talk you out of it; they'll question your motives and generally do all manner of things to dissuade you. Not everyone. But enough to give you pause for self-doubt.

Don't let it freeze you. Simply understand that when you step out of your comfort zone you make other people feel uncomfortable too.

That's okay. Don't get mad. Live with it. It's a human reaction. You never know – you might have done the same in their shoes.

But don't live your life by other people's limitations.

...And now also embrace the fact that you will also be criticized for the right reasons.

Suck it up. If you get constructive criticism about your business plans, your painting style, your dreams of promotion, your travel plan then don't dismiss it.

Weigh up the merits of that criticism; they might have a point. And this sort of criticism can make your plans better.

In other words, you need to distinguish between constructive criticism and that which comes from someone else's fear and discomfort.

Dealing with criticism

What would you say in response to the following criticisms?

1. "You'll never stick to it. I bet you give up."

2. "You don't have the knowledge / skills to do what you want to do."

3. "You'll neglect other commitments and / or people in your life."

4. "You can't afford to do that. It'll cost too much."

5. "It'll never work."

6. "You haven't thought it through properly."

7. "You're not doing it for the right reasons."

8. "No one is going to be interested in what you're offering."

9. "I don't approve of what you're going to do."

How to turn criticism into constructive criticism and how to respond to criticism. Constructively.

Each of the responses below is a way to turn a criticism into a request for constructive advice.

Each response is appropriate for one or more of the criticisms listed previously. See if you can match a response with a criticism.

- Can you tell me what I might have missed?

- What it is I need to think about?

- I'm sorry to hear that.

- What do you think should be the right reasons?

- Why do you think that?

- In what ways will I be neglectful, do you think?

- What is it you think I need to know or be able to do?

And here's a few more phrases you might find useful:

- What would you suggest?

- What would you do if you were me?

- What improvements would you suggest?

"You can't stay in your corner of the forest waiting for people to come to you. You have to go to them sometimes."

Winnie the Pooh

saddle up

The world is not conspiring against you. (It just feels like that. Sometimes.) Some advice for the "persecuted"

Since we're being honest. Do you suffer from "Poor Me" syndrome, a persecution complex? Is that what's stopping you from scratching your itch?

Some people think they can't do it because the world is against them. It isn't. It's kind of against everyone.

But for some people this sense of persecution can be crippling. The philosopher and mathematician Bertrand Russell[8] developed four rules to keep persecution mania at bay:

1. "Don't overestimate your own merits"
If no-one likes your paintings or your business plan then consider that maybe they're right and you're not very good. In a hundred years we'll know whether it was a waste of good canvas or you really were "afflicted by the desire to produce unrecognized masterpieces".

If it seems that perhaps your friends are right then admittedly it is painful to accept that your merits are not what you hoped. But recognizing this now – rather than thinking the world is out to get you – means you can move on, rebuild, reframe your objectives and start again with targets and achievements you can succeed at.

2. "Don't expect others to take as much interest in you as you do yourself"

Don't expect too much of other people. Everyone has their own ego, their own needs. If others bend over backwards to help you it may be that you are asking too much of them and not that they are being too selfish. The problem might be your own ego.

3. "Remember that your motives are not always as altruistic as they seem to yourself"

Those who believe their "itch" has a higher moral calling are especially likely to feel persecuted. After all, a mission with a higher altruistic component ought perhaps to command extra special support...not indifference or criticism. It might be true that you have greater altruism than your compadres.

But maybe you should just double-check your motives.

"People who have a high opinion of their own moral excellence," suggests Russell, are not being honest with themselves. As a consequence they are in grave danger of feeling persecuted when others question the motives behind their actions.

4. "Don't imagine that most people give enough thought to you to have any special desire to persecute you"

Normal people do not spend their waking hours plotting how to thwart you. They're too busy trying to pay their mortgage and working out why their boiler is making a funny sound. Thinking that you are important enough to have been singled out by unseen forces to be squashed, ignored, or always get parking tickets is based on a vanity that you have special importance in the world.

But start doing something special and that might change...

COMMITTED
BIG TALKERS AND
DAY DREAMERS

Bravo, this is your stop

Maybe you're quite happy to stick at being a big talker about the thing you want to start rather being the sort of person who actually goes and does it.

That's okay. There's a lot of folk like that about.

As the comedian George Burns said:

"Too bad that all the people who know how to run the country are busy driving taxis or cutting hair."

There's no denying that it's fun talking about what you would do.

But bear in mind that you might start to wear out the patience of other people.

If you spot gritted teeth or bleeding ears whenever you start talking about your grand plans that you've no intention of ever starting:

"Talk doesn't cook rice."

Chinese proverb

Now then.

The rest of the book is for those that want to convert hot air into dynamism and demolish all the different ways you might stop yourself from starting what you want to do and scratching your itch...

PART 3

FEAR AND REGRET

"He who is not courageous enough to take risks will accomplish nothing in life."

Muhammad Ali

"Twenty years from now you will be more disappointed by the things that you didn't do than by the ones you did do. So throw off the bowlines. Sail away from the safe harbour. Catch the trade winds in your sails. Explore. Dream. Discover."

Mark Twain

When it comes to seizing control of your life and turning your talk into action what stops most people is fear. Fear has its place. Our ancestors had a finely tuned sense of fear which leapt into life the moment they heard a twig snap.

Well that was designed for the day when the bad news was being eaten by a dinosaur. Now the bad news is you might not get promoted, someone might not buy from your sandwich shop, or you might even get sacked from a job you don't much care for.

Regret that you never sought promotion or showed anyone your paintings will hurt you more.

Embrace the fear and leave regret for some other sucker.

Embrace the fear and leave regret for some other sucker.

The scales that matter the most

Regret weighs more than Fear. But fear looks bigger. That's because you can see it standing there in front of you. Daring you. Taunting you.

Regret that you didn't follow your heart to do what you felt compelled to do sneaks up on you over time.

And every year regret grows heavier.

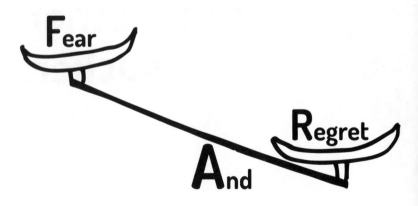

...Which is to say what you should be really scared of is regret. Regretting what you might have done but never did.

If you do the thing and make a mistake there's always the opportunity to salvage things by taking a different course or more action.

But regret is much harder to resolve. Regret reaches a long claw from the past and lowers a cold hand on your shoulder today. If you failed to do something in the past when you had the chance...then that remains the case forever. You can't turn back time.

Once you appreciate the immense dread that you ought to have for regret then many or all of your other fears will diminish in proportion and you will start doing.

Fear regret...and by doing so, discover your courage to do your "thing" whatever that might be.

What's stopping you / what are you frightened of?

For each question, tick one or more statements that apply to you.

1. You work in an office but you're tired of sitting behind a desk. You want a job where you'll be more active. However, you:

a. Had thought a job in an office was what you wanted and it's not. You worry you are about to make another wrong choice. ☐

---

b. Find it difficult to explain and justify to others what you want to do. ☐

---

c. Will probably earn less money. ☐

---

d. Are put off by the need to re-train. You never were any good at studying. ☐

---

e. Would have to give up your 9 – 5 routine and weekends off. ☐

---

f. Have to work longer hours. ☐

2. You've always wanted to perform (music, singing, acting, stand up comedian perhaps?) but are put off by the unpredictable income. Now, thanks to your partner's recent pay rise and their encouragement you can just about afford to do it. You:

a. Recall that your partner has lost their job before and wonder if it'll happen again while you're still trying to make it. ☐

b. Imagine people will think you're taking advantage of your partner's position. ☐

c. Worry that you won't be able to afford your current lifestyle on a smaller income. ☐

d. Lack confidence because you don't have any formal training. ☐

e. Dismiss the idea. You have a good job which you quite enjoy and you think you should just perform on the side. ☐

f. Are put off by the idea of probably having to work into the early hours. ☐

3. You've been offered redundancy from your marketing job. This could be the perfect opportunity to pursue your dream of becoming an interior designer. You:

a. Shy away from the prospect of starting at the bottom of the ladder again. ☐

b. Worry that other people will say you're too old now to compete with young, hip creative types. ☐

c. Worry you'd have to make the redundancy money last a long time while you studied. ☐

d. Will only do it if you can get into one of the best art colleges. ☐

e. Think you should just get another job in marketing because it's what you know and what you do well. ☐

f. Realize you'd still have to work part time as well as study interior design. There won't be enough hours in the day. ☐

4. The business you started on the side is actually starting to take off! So much so, you could probably leave your job. You:

a. Worry if you really have the skills to run a business; you've got yourself in a mess with money in the past. ☐

b. Remember the people who originally doubted your idea. Now they'll think you're mad to give up your day job. ☐

c. Balk at the idea of being solely responsible for your income. ☐

d. Think there must be a lot to learn; courses you'd need to attend. ☐

e. Think this could just be a blip and the success won't last. Best to leave it as a sideline. ☐

f. Worry that if the business then became even more successful you'd be overwhelmed and unable to cope. ☐

5. You tell a colleague you've always wanted to write a novel. They ask you when you're going to get started. You:

a. Explain you've heard that so many writers before you have found it impossible to find a publisher. ☐

b. Worry that colleagues will think you're not fully committed to your job. ☐

c. Explain it's a historical novel and you couldn't afford to travel places for the background research. ☐

d. Explain that you don't have an A level or degree in English. ☐

e. Are anxious about putting yourself out there and then discover you're no good. You'd actually like to keep it as a dream. ☐

f. Don't want to give up all your spare time and other interests. ☐

6. You work for a small company that's rapidly expanding. Your boss is leaving – you'd love her job. You:

a. Have stepped up to something big before and it was far too stressful and you had to back down. ☐

b. Deny your interest. You don't want to appear grasping. ☐

c. Worry it might mean moving to London in future and you couldn't afford to live there, even on the increased salary. ☐

d. Compare yourself with your boss. She has a first class degree. You're not that clever. ☐

e. Know you should register your interest and know it makes career sense but you do actually like your current position. ☐

f. Are put off by the fact that you'd have to work longer hours. ☐

Results: If you ticked:

Mostly a. You're trapped by the past

Mostly b. You feel held back by other people's opinions

Mostly c. You're worried about money

Mostly d. You're held back by your education. Or lack of it

Mostly e. You're trapped by what you have

Mostly f. You feel you're too busy and there aren't enough hours in the day

Now you have acknowledged your fears, it's time to flush them away...

How to flush away your fears

Recognize your fears for what they are: mere excuses not to grasp for your dreams. Hold them up to the light and examine them.

Be logical and rational not emotional. What do they really mean? Is it enough to stop you in your tracks? Forever? Or are you seeing things that aren't really there?

> ## "A black cat crossing your path signifies that the animal is going somewhere."
>
> Groucho Marx

FEAR #1:

THE PAST

The prison you accidentally created.

So you made mistakes in the past. Get over it. Don't dwell on it. The more you dwell on something the bigger it becomes.

Instead, recognize that we all make mistakes. The only way to prevent those mistakes blocking you from entering the ring is to acknowledge them, learn from them and move on.

Unless you're perfect you have accumulated "baggage" in your life. Whatever it is you need to deal with it. Because it won't go away and no-one else is going to deal with it.

Running away from problems doesn't make them go away.

The sooner you deal with them, the sooner they are dealt with. If you don't do it, who will? It's much easier to bury our heads in the sand, but we have to pull them out at some point and when we do the problem will just be a whole lot bigger.

The decision you are about to make is the intersection between your past and your future...

The National Archives in Washington DC is where the US Constitution, the Bill of Rights and other historic documents are preserved. These documents define the USA's past.

There's a quotation that captures better than any other the importance of history in bringing a country or a person to the state they find themselves in at any given moment.

From a statue outside the building to a commemorative series of postage stamps this quotation runs through the organization like words on a stick of Brighton rock.

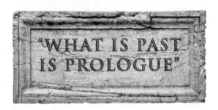

The quotation is from Shakespeare's play, *The Tempest*.

Two of the characters are about to commit a murder. Their past – every action they took and every decision they have ever made – leads them to the point of killing someone. Or not. Needless to say, they cannot change their history...but their future is theirs to make.

The past, with its baggage and mistakes, is nothing but the lead up to every current decision. If you're reading this book then you probably believe in free will.

Every decision is yours to make.
To do or not to do.

The past is past. The limit of history is NOW. All you can choose now is your next move...

...Be sure to understand the significance:

Don't let your past mistakes control your future.

Letting go of the past

1. Take a piece of paper and on the left, write down what past events, experiences and mistakes are making you hesitate and might be holding you back.

2. On the right, write down the reasons you wrote on page 31 about why now is the right time for you to start doing what you want to do.

3. Cut the piece of paper in half. Place the paper with the reasons from the past on the floor behind you. Place the paper with the reason for doing what you want to do in front of you.

The only way to let go of the past is to focus on the future. Keep your focus on what's written in front of you!

FEAR #2:

OTHER PEOPLE'S OPINION: FEAR OF RIDICULE

Do you worry people will laugh at you for trying to chase your dream?

Big deal.

a) So what if they do?

b) If someone laughs at you for trying then question whether such a person deserves even a standing ticket in your life story. Let them go; show them the exit.

c) Although, having kicked them outside into the rain the fact is they're doing you a favour. The good thing about people laughing at you is it stops you taking yourself too seriously. Actually, you should laugh too. 106 billion people have taken themselves seriously so far and what good has it done them?

d) Incidentally the person mocking you is 72.8% water.

That's like being bullied by a bath tub. So what do they know?
(And come to that, how seriously are you taking yourself, you drip?)

> "It behooves every man to remember that the work of the critic is of altogether secondary importance, and that in the end, progress is accomplished by the man who does things."
>
> Theodore Roosevelt, 26th American President

The opinions of others and what you can learn from wearing a Barry Manilow T-shirt

It's a tragic story as far as Barry Manilow is concerned but fascinating for the rest of us. In an experiment 50% of students, who were required to walk into a room full of other students while wearing a T-shirt emblazoned with Barry Manilow's face, felt that half the room had immediately clocked the embarrassingly uncool item. The truth is only 20% had noticed it. The same error was true if they wore a T-shirt with a "cool" image of Bob Marley, Martin Luther King or the comedian Jerry Seinfeld. The experiment showed that people think the world is paying more attention to what they're doing than they really are. We're all egomaniacs, people!! The world is not standing by ready to ridicule us. They're busy trying to get on with their own lives.[9]

So get on with yours!

FEAR #3:

DOUGH AND D'OH!
SO YOU'RE SHORT OF MONEY...

That might not be a bad thing.

Sure it's easy to say, but here's why: If you're earning a zillion bucks in a bank shifting money around the world then no-one doubts that it's easier to buy, for example, that polo pony and start your new sport. But money is a double-edged sword which people become addicted to and which makes it harder for them to quit their job and start what they really want to do.

High earners get trapped by their lifestyle. Wall Street and the City of London are teeming with folk who vowed to make a pile of money, quick and young, save it up and quit to do something they enjoyed: pig farming, fashion styling, acting ...but then found they couldn't give up.

This isn't to say you should shed tears for the wealthy. But you should recognize a certain liberty to do what you want: you have less to lose!

For example, if you're young then you can (maybe) go sleep on a friend's sofa and work night shifts in a bar to fund your passion developing a business or an artistic career. That's not so easy to do if you think life's about paying off the loans on your Porsche and penthouse suite.

How can you fund what you want to do?

Do your research! Find out about:

☐ Bank loans and government loans

☐ Crowdfunding

☐ Charities or trusts that provide loans or grants. If, for example, you are a former member of the Armed Forces, Help For Heroes and the British Legion may be able to help.

☐ Renting out a room in your home. Take in a lodger, a student. Rent a room or your flat or house to tourists – see www. airbnb.com

☐ Teaching what you know and can do and charge other people for lessons.

☐ And finally, ask family and friends if they might lend or even give you some money – though be warned, this is NOT likely to be the easiest route to take!

FEAR #4:

EDUKASHUN
YOU WENT TO THE WRONG SCHOOL OR YOU DIDN'T GO TO SCHOOL

A bit like money, the great schools help. And if you got a second-rate education it's tempting to question whether the cards are so stacked against you it would be pointless to even start the fight.

That would be wrong.

Just ask Bill Gates, Richard Branson, Coco Chanel or even Simon Cowell.

Bill Gates never finished university. Richard Branson not only left school at 16, but he was dyslexic to boot – a good excuse if you needed one. Coco Chanel was an orphan from 12 and had no formal education and Simon Cowell started his working life in a mail room.

25% of Forbes wealthiest Americans never graduated from college.

Proof that your attitude, not your education, is what counts.

Sure, going to the "right" school may open a few doors, but it's you, not your education, that will keep them open.

FEAR #5:

TRAPPED BY WHAT YOU HAVE

If you're thinking that you don't want to risk what you have in order to pursue your itch then perhaps the surprising truth is you're pretty happy with what you have. In that case embrace what you have and enjoy it more.

Maybe, for example, the job is OK and what makes you unhappy is the fact you don't play sport anymore. Again – you need to analyze yourself honestly.

Maybe you'd be foolish to rock the boat.

Blaming your job may be an outlet for your frustration that something else is preventing you buying a pair of tennis shoes and getting back out on court.

In contrast you might consider it thoughtfully and conclude that what you have isn't enough and maybe it never was.

Maybe you've outgrown the job, the relationship, the town you live in...

If you decide you don't like it any more then cast off your fears and Rock That Boat.

FEAR #6:

THERE AREN'T ENOUGH HOURS IN THE DAY

True. There aren't. And that's never going to change.

But if you're a doer you'll recognize that we all get the same amount of time in a day, it's how we use it that matters.

Which means you are just going to have to get smart about how you prioritize time.

Consider also that the aspect of time you ought to be motivated by is the part that you can't manage – and that's how fast it's flowing past.

So deal with the bits that you can.

Prioritize!

FEAR #7:

I'M TOO BUSY!
THIS IS THE TWIN SISTER OF FEAR #6.

Believing yourself to be monumentally and eye-poppingly busy may be an accurate reflection of your life. It may also be another way of hiding from the act of getting started.

Amid the cacophony of your busyness you may have had time to hear the term "a busy fool". As far as this book is concerned this simply means you can be extremely busy doing the wrong thing purely for the purpose of being too busy to confront and do what you really need to do.

By the same token, another well-worn phrase among business leaders is: "If you need something done give the task to a busy person." Someone who is already really busy doing important things doesn't have time to prevaricate and delay. They have to prioritize the important stuff and get things done.

If this is an excuse that rings bells for you then you should stop and take stock. Make sure your busy behaviour is pointed in the right direction.

To paraphrase Stephen Covey, the author of *The 7 Habits of Highly Effective People* –

there's no point busily climbing the ladder if your ladder's leaning against the wrong wall.

What your week looks like

Fill in the following timetable with all the commitments and activities you do in a typical week.

Then, use different coloured highlighters to highlight:

1. What's important, a priority and non-negotiable

2. What you can delegate

3. What you can drop

4. Where you might have some extra time

	Monday	Tuesday	Wednesday
6–8am			
8–10am			
10am–12pm			
12–2pm			
2–4pm			
4–6pm			
6–8pm			
8–10pm			
10pm–12am			

Thursday	Friday	Saturday	Sunday

Five ways to stop being so busy and get things done: Optimize!

1. Are you a morning, afternoon or evening person?
What's the optimum time of day for you? If you're not sure, try out different times of day on various activities to see when you have the most mental and physical energy.

2. Think about what the optimum amount of time is that you can focus on doing things. Be clear about what sort of jobs or activities you can only spend a short time on and which ones you can spend a long time on.

3. Try short bursts. It may be that 3 separate sessions of 20 minutes focused attention, with 5 minute breaks between each session, could be better for you than one long 60 minute slog. Try the "short bursts" technique and see if it works for you.

4. Compromise. Your life may not make it easy for you to do things at your optimum times of day. Try and be flexible and work out the best compromise possible.

5. Avoid interruptions. If you know that the afternoon is your most productive time of day – stand firm and don't let yourself to be distracted or interrupted.

On the subject of being too busy, how there are not enough hours in the day and why it is important to plan the campaign to scratch your itch, consider the 18th-century life of Benjamin Franklin.

Franklin was one of 17 children. He was the really busy one; he knew something about managing his time. One of the things he did in his life was to invent the lightning rod. And another was to create the first public lending library in America. In fact he's also the face on the $100 dollar bill, which is why that note is nicknamed a "Benjamin". Perhaps he's more famous for being one of the founding fathers of the United States of America, which is to say he was one of the authors of the American Constitution as well as the Declaration of Independence.

Franklin was a newspaper editor, too. And he was also the first US ambassador to France. He created the first fire service in Pennsylvania. He invented bifocals. And he was once the Governor of Pennsylvania. He charted and named the Atlantic sea current we know today as the Gulf Stream. Even when he toyed around he was productive and he is a member of the US Chess Hall of Fame.

Here is his daily schedule as he described it in his autobiography. It is a great example of setting goals, planning your time but not overplanning, measuring your goals and getting things done.

The morning question, What good shall I do this day?	5	Rise, wash, and address *Powerful Goodness*; contrive day's business and take the resolution of the day; prosecute the present study; and breakfast.
	6	
	7	
	8	
	9	Work.
	10	
	11	
	12	Read or overlook my accounts, and dine.
	1	
	2	
	3	Work.
	4	
	5	
	6	Put things in their places, supper, music, or diversion, or conversation; examination of the day.
	7	
	8	
Evening question, What good have I done today?	9	
	10	
	11	
	12	
	1	Sleep.
	2	
	3	
	4	

The discomfort zone

If all this talk of confronting your fears makes you uncomfortable then congratulations: you're in the right place.

It means you are toppling forward out of your armchair and into the world of action.

Deliberately aim for the Discomfort zone.

The Eurofighter is one of the most unstable planes in the sky. That's what you get after spending tens of billions of pounds developing a state-of-the-art airplane.

It is one of the fifth generation of fighter jets. And these cutting edge aircraft were built to be unstable.

Of course it's not called being unstable. It's called Relaxed Stability. But the point is the plane can flip over, up, sideways, skip upwards, zip downwards in response to the tiniest instruction from the pilot.

The boffins couldn't even make planes this unstable until they had invented "fly by wire" technology. Fly by wire means the pilot flies by sending electronic signals to motors on the wings and tail of the plane which continually adjust the plane's state in the air. Before this flying planes was a lot more manual.

In fifth-generation relaxed stability jet fighters the plane's computer makes all the adjustments. A pilot simply couldn't keep the plane in the air without the computers making thousands and thousands of micro-adjustments all the time.

So why did they build jets that cost $100 million each and are inherently unstable – and almost unflyable?

It's because the giddy instability is what makes the plane so extravagantly manoeuvrable. A small push on the joystick this way or that and the fighter can make turns and loops that would have been impossible in their old planes, which suddenly seemed slow and dull.

The hard thing with the Eurofighter isn't swooping, turning and looping; the hard thing was staying on the same old course.

Well that's what all the previous generations of jet fighters were like.

They could fly in really mean straight lines and predictable curves. And they were much easier to fly. But those pilots in their comfortable old fighters, in their armchairs, didn't stand a chance against the pilots who were in the discomfort zone.

This is where you win. Outside the comfort zone.

The discomfort zone is a state you'll need to pass through to achieve any change of significance.

Here's a yogi who has turned a bed of nails into an environment for relaxation and meditation.

Each to their own.

Dig deep

There's always a reason not to do something. The truth is for many of us, life can be hard at times, but this is when we have to dig deep and push forward. We have to move away from our comfort zone and create solutions where none seem to exist.

J.K. Rowling was a single mum when she wrote Harry Potter.

Not only that, but she had to face being turned down by countless publishers before one would believe in her. It would have been much easier for her to have said, "I'm a single mum, I just don't have the money or time to do this," but she didn't.

And where is she now? A billionaire fulfilling her life's ambitions of being one of the most successful authors of all time.

Yes, it is harder if you are a single parent or have challenging family commitments, but there is a big difference between "harder" and impossible.

You have to do whatever it takes and don't give up. Find another single mum (or dad) to share childcare with, work nights, find something you can do working from home in the first instance. Whatever you do, it probably won't be what you want to do, but it's not supposed to be – it's supposed to be a stepping stone to get you where you want to go.

Many people have a different type of family commitment – obligation. Parents want the best for their children, but this can often mean pushing them down a path that isn't for them.

How many people do you know who are in careers because at some point in their life they thought it would please their parents, spouse, career teacher or society?

We have to be true to ourselves whilst managing these obstacles sensitively. Explain and prove to those that love you that following your own path doesn't mean a life of debauchery and destitution; OK, you may not do the Ph.D. or become a doctor, but you're going to be happy and fulfilled and ultimately that's all any parent wants – even if they can't always see it at the time.

Then there's the age-old excuse of…age. Too young, too old.

Jordan Romero was 9 when he climbed Kilimanjaro.

Colonel Sanders was 40 before he started cooking his famous chicken – out of his dining room! And it wasn't until he was 65 that he started franchising one of the world's most famous fast food restaurants, Kentucky Fried Chicken.

You can always find an excuse, but you can always find an inspiration too.

If man can land on the moon, there's not much you can't do once you've made your mind up and moved from talking about it to actually doing it.

So get resourceful. Accept the fact that you may have more challenges than most. It happens. But you have just the same chance of success.

Give up the TV. Wake up an hour earlier. Steal time from wherever you can. Enlist the help and support of all your family and friends. Make a public commitment to your goals and not only will it give you an extra impetus to achieve them but it also gathers support and momentum behind you.

And as we explain on page 192, holding yourself publicly accountable is proven to greatly increase your chance of success.

So keep digging, digging, digging, digging...

And dig deep.

Final word on fear:

If you're not feeling a little bit apprehensive about what you're about to do then it probably doesn't matter much anyway.

You should be feeling like this.

> "Inside of a ring or out, ain't nothing wrong with going down. It's staying down that's wrong."
>
> Muhammad Ali

Regret

Since you're the sort of person who has chosen to read this book then probably there's not much need to say more about regret. You "get" it. The utter horror of regret will be clear to you.

You can't change the past – once the moment is gone and the opportunity has passed by and been squandered, if at that point, you didn't climb inside the ropes well…then you didn't.

Tough luck, you have to deal with it.

On the other hand if you did surmount your fears and try to tackle your itch and things got smashed and spilled in the process then you can deal with the consequences today.

Action is how you change things; fix things; do things.

> "Act. Or be acted upon."
>
> Anon
>
> "To fight fear, act.
> To increase fear – wait,
> put off, postpone."
>
> David Joseph Schwartz

Here's a simple example of how fear can be paralyzing and turn into regret:

Anyone who has ever wanted to chat to a speaker after a conference, or chat up an attractive stranger at a party will know the best thing is to act immediately.

And you'll know that if you hang around waiting then it gets harder and harder as the opportunity loses its momentum, the initiative evaporates, you get tongue-tied and you begin to consider the other option which is just to skip the whole idea and carry on as you were. That begins to seem easier and easier.

Eventually you take that option.

And what changes?

Nothing.

Don't kid yourself you're doing when you're not:

...Shopping isn't doing.

But it feels a bit like it.

So does researching.

So does tweeting.

And so does talking about it.

It's all Jaw Jaw.

In fact you can kid yourself a thousand ways that you're doing when in truth you're not.

But you will be found out eventually – when you get the pang of regret that you never did what you wanted to.

Doing is the route to fulfillment – at least fulfillment of the goals that will stop that damn itching!

Sidestep regret: invest yourself in doing and find the route to happiness!

A study by the psychologists Leaf van Boven and Thomas Gilovich[10] required participants to:

a/ rate the happiness they received from experiences such as going to the theatre, the cinema, the ski slopes, traveling and going out to dinner.

And

b/ rate the happiness they got from buying things like TVs, stereos, computers, clothes and jewellery.

Well, you know where this is going: the doing made people happier than the having.

But wait, there's more.

It turns out that even when people were asked to think of an experience, they felt happier than when they were asked to think about having bought something.

Now imagine how much greater the satisfaction would be if the experience was something that had great personal value.

If it had been a mission. If it had been the scratching of a lifelong itch!

...Oh, and in the words of Steve Jobs: "One more thing":

Gilovich and co. also found that when people listened to one person talk about something special they had done and another talk about something special they had bought, the person who was liked the most would be the doer not the haver.

So next time you're passing one of Steve Jobs' Apple stores or a shoe shop and are about to burn up your precious cash: think twice. Tie yourself to the mast like Odysseus and fix your aim on DOING not HAVING!!

Be like Odysseus:

Don't be distracted by sirens or BUYING stuff...
Tie yourself to your mission of DOING stuff.

"Ulysses and the Sirens" (1891) by John William Waterhouse (1849–1917)

Odysseus, the mythological adventurer, wanted to hear the mesmerizing song of the Sirens, the evil bird-women who happened to have achingly beautiful voices.

But this was surely a suicide wish because the song of the Sirens was infamously irresistible and had lured countless sailors to their deaths on the rocky shores of the islands where they lived.

But you don't get to sack the city of Troy without being a plucky and ingenious chap. And Odysseus was determined to hear the Siren song without meeting his maker. So he had all the men on his boat block their ears (but not his) with beeswax so they couldn't hear the song.

Then he ordered them to tie him to the mast and not to untie him until they had passed by the islands.

And once in range he begged the men to untie him so he could get closer to the islands and the music. The men steadfastly refused until they had long sailed away from the Sirens. And thus he was able to survive the temptations. And go on to do more heroic derring-do.

So next time the siren song of consumer product fetishism grabs you, you know what to do. Fix your eyes on the goal and be prepared to resist the inevitable temptations to falter along the way.

Sample pictures of graffiti in a few adjacent streets in Central London.

Another sign that the world is not what it was: Take street art (or graffiti – choose your preferred word): Artists such as Banksy from Bristol in the UK or the Faile collective from New York can now command huge prices in art galleries around the world.

The idea that graffiti is the product of work-shy layabouts is outdated. A vast amount of the cynical "messages" contained in street art warns us not to be coerced by advertising into finding our goals in consumption but instead to go and DO.

We've been trained by generations of Mad Men, marketers and advertisers to want THINGS.

This is bad counsel.

Rebel.

Instead DO.

Invest in DOING – learning, training, experimenting, writing, travelling, helping, building businesses, realizing dreams!

Before they were called marketers, these masters of manipulation were known as consumption engineers.[11]

PART 4

START

"You can't expect to hit the jackpot if you don't put a few nickels in the machine."

Flip Wilson

If this book were the Bible the first commandment would be:
Start.

If it were a cookery book it would say:
Add lots and lots of Go to the mix.

If it were a car manual it would say:
The vehicle won't move until you turn the ignition.

But it's not. That's why it says:
Don't be a chicken. The instant you cross that start line everything changes.

Let's Roll

It's impossible to overstate the importance of starting.

As it's the be all and end all of this book you might wonder why we haven't got to this point until now. Maybe it should have been at the START?

That's a fair question. So here's why:

Most people don't start until they realize:

a. They've got an itch
b. It's natural and right to have fears yet understand that reason can keep these fears in check
c. Everyone has their own unique challenges
d. They'd rather tackle their fears than live for eternity with the regret of losing their bottle and not doing

The good news is that the mere act of starting is what makes things change. Starting is itself a guarantee of success because it means you are already saying farewell to the status quo.

...And finally you will recall that we started the book with
e. The rapid passage of time

Time is the imperative. The whooshing by of time, like the rise and fall of the sun, is the one certainty.

Time is your spur to get up and act.

And that's why you have to start now.

Climb into the ring.

The Elimination of Procrastination

Of course, you feel the urge to procrastinate. That's only human.

You see, scratching the itch – doing anything worthwhile – takes an investment in time and effort and the rewards are in the future.

In the meantime your vices are offering you immediate short-term satisfaction: put on a DVD, have a glass of wine, listen to some music, surf the Internet, lie on the sofa, raid the fridge...do them all at once!

This battle between your vices and your virtue is as old as the hills and the outcome is just as predictable unless you are determined and smart.

To help you concentrate on doing and ignore the temptations of procrastination here are some tips from Professor Piers Steel who studies procrastination at the University of Calgary.[12]

- Sully tempting alternatives: imagine as vividly as possible the downside of being tempted by distraction.

  Imagine the TV remote is tacky with the paw-prints of your permanently ill young nieces; that the TV is wired badly and will explode if you switch on during the day; that the door to the fridge will fall off if you open it as often during the day as you usually do… You get the picture.

- Focus on the abstract aspects of temptations: triple chocolate cheesecake, for example, can be construed as its constituent parts of fat and sugar…and that doesn't sound so yummy.

- Entirely eliminate cues that remind you of distracting alternatives. Keeping your workplace free of clutter will help you accomplish this.

- Replace the clutter with meaningful messages or images. The legendary hotelier Conrad Hilton kept a photograph of the Waldorf Hotel on his desk to help him maintain his focus and avoid distraction and procrastination. The photo was there for 18 years… until he bought the hotel.

- Try to physically compartmentalize your work life and your leisure by keeping them as far away as possible. If you work from home you need to mentally compartmentalize the activities.

A picture on a desk...

...helped provide unshakeable focus and zero
distractions for 18 years

...and this brought Conrad Hilton the prize

"Never put off till tomorrow, what you can do the day after tomorrow."

Mark Twain

...It's amusing but as advice goes it's not great

"The secret of getting ahead is getting started. The secret of getting started is breaking your complex overwhelming tasks into small manageable tasks, and then starting on the first one."

Mark Twain

...Not so amusing but great advice

Your internal nagging friend

Here's some good news.

Once you start something the subconscious brain won't let you stop. So you'll have your own internal slave-driver whipping you on.

It's called the Zeigarnik[13] effect. A Russian psychologist, Bluma Zeigarnik, was intrigued to learn that waiters could take complicated orders from a large group of students and remember them perfectly without writing them down.

But as soon as the bill had been paid waiters' memories of what had been ordered fell apart.

It was as if the order was put into the mental trash can.

Her conclusion was that once a project had been set running the subconscious was keeping constant track of it and would badger the waiter to make sure it got completed. It was as if any interruption to a task becomes a psychic disturbance that unsettles the brain.

What this means is that simply by starting and committing to your project you get a little help – in the form of your subconscious – to nag you and ensure you get "closure" in psychological terms. In our terms it's ensuring you do the next big thing. Which is finishing the task!

That's one to take away.

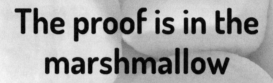

The proof is in the marshmallow

(...why STARTING is a great way to SUCCEED)

Some of the brightest and most successful people in business have tried this test. It's called the Marshmallow Challenge.[14]

This is how it goes:

- You work in teams of four.
- Each team is given 20 sticks of spaghetti, a yard of tape and a yard of string.
- And a marshmallow.
- Each team has 18 minutes to build the tallest structure they can. The marshmallow must be on the top.

Simple, right?

The challenge was devised by designer Peter Skillman and it has since been used by innovation expert Tom Wujec in his studies of how senior executives collaborate and innovate.

But what's interesting to we doers, is what the experiment has to say about the value of starting.

Q: Who did Wujec find were among the worst performing groups of people?

A: Recent graduates of business school. Only slightly better were CEOs of large organizations.

Q: Which group of people were among the top performers?

A: Kindergarten kids. Their spaghetti and marshmallow structures averaged almost three times the height of the MBA grads.

The reason the kids succeeded while their older and more educated rivals failed was they just kept doing. The MBA grads discussed plans and roles and responsibilities and postured (and maybe wrote a mission statement, who knows?) and then finally, as time ran out, scrambled to build a tower of spaghetti and place a marshmallow on top only to find at the last minute – ta-dah! – that the weight of the marshmallow collapsed the structure.

Meanwhile, the kids – being kids – just went right ahead and got practical. Which means they simply started trying to build a structure right from the whistle and pretty quickly found out what worked and didn't work. No fear of failure. No hesitation. Just doing.

The professionals have a word for it

What the kids were doing in the marshmallow challenge was "rapid prototyping".

And what's good enough for kids with marshmallows is good enough for big business.

It's a similar approach to that which has been widely adopted for many software and internet development projects. It's called LEAN development.

Teams of software developers used to spend years locked in a bunker writing code so that one fine day they could come blinking into the sunlight and announce to the world: "Come, see! Here's our new computer program!" At which point they might discover a flaw in the user experience or a slew of bugs. Dang!

Nowadays, teams try to get new versions of code written every week or even every day. That's how they discover problems faster. And it's how they steal the competitive advantage over their rivals.

They start doing and move their ideas from the hypothetical to the real as fast as possible.

They move from the stationary talking position to the dynamic action position. No fear. No regrets.

And importantly they move closer to success with every iteration.

The history of accidental success

When you start you don't know where you'll finish. You could call that "risk".

This uncertainty of outcome is one of the reasons some people get paralyzed by fear at the thought of moving from the talking state to the doing state.

But perhaps it doesn't matter whether you get direct from A to Z.

It might be that ending up at F is still a great result.

History is, after all, littered with great tales of people who began one thing only to discover another great thing, which they would never have done otherwise. And in retrospect it doesn't seem like a failure.

In fact what it tells us is that the thing is simply to start.

Coca-Cola was originally developed as a medicine that promised to cure anything from hysteria to headaches.

In 1968 the scientist Dr. Spencer Silver at 3M figured he had discovered something of little worth until one of his colleagues said he found the "low tack" adhesive useful to bookmark his Bible. Shortly after the ubiquitous Post-It note was born.

The short distance between the Atlantic and the Pacific oceans was accidentally discovered by Spanish conquistadors searching for gold.[15] Now it has been developed into the Panama Canal which reduces a boat trip from New York to San Francisco from 14,000 miles to 5,900 miles.

The multi-platinum selling musician Jack Johnson wanted to be a professional surfer. In fact he was a very good surfer, but at just 17, an accident put an end to his dreams and his future no longer looked so certain. Still unsure of what to do, he went to film school and it was there that he started playing music and soon realized he was an even better guitarist than surfer. And the rest, as they say, is history.

To celebrate the World Fair coming to Paris in 1887–9 architects were invited to build a temporary structure. The competition rules required that the winning structure should be easily dismantled after 20 years. Nevertheless, the Eiffel Tower is still standing over 120 years after winning the contest. More recently the London Eye, the enormous ferris wheel on the south bank of London's River Thames, was constructed to be a temporary celebration of the 2000 millennium, and this too is still around. The key thing of course is that people with drive and vision got them started.

Harrison Ford, an actor whose career was stalling, retrained as a carpenter and got a job building cabinets at the home of George Lucas. Whereas staying put trying to get acting jobs didn't work for him, striking out in a new direction did. Lucas got him to read some lines for actors auditioning for parts in his 1977 film *Star Wars*. The carpenter and ex-actor convinced Lucas to give him the key role of Han Solo and a superstar was born.

The solace of failure

Suppose you wanted to be the chef who started something like this:

And to do it you quit your job here:

But it didn't work out.

And instead of doing:

...you own this shack and work hard seven days a week:

Then did you fail? Well, it depends. None of these outcomes is necessarily a failure (or a success). They're just different answers to the question: Where do you want be?

But if you didn't like where you were to begin with then the act of pursuing your dream means wherever you end up, it will be somewhere different. Falling short of your target or changing direction can still be a success.

How to surprise someone

Do what you say.

Seriously. We are so used to people promising the earth and delivering a flop that the one sure way to surprise and delight someone is simply to do what you say you will when you say you will.

And the person you will please the most will be you.

Spot the difference...

'Nuff said?

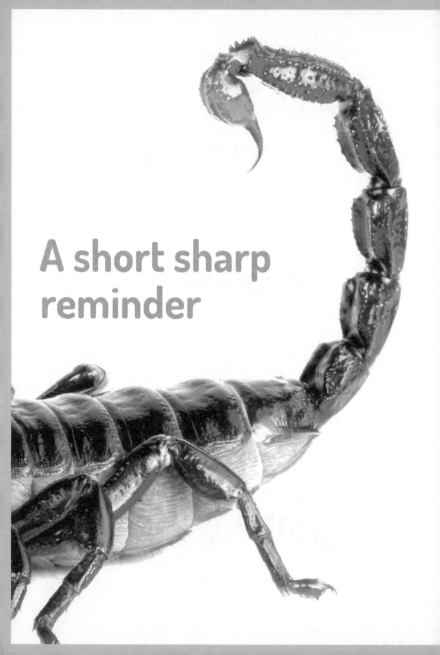

A short sharp reminder

...about that sting in the tail

If having considered all of the above:

That is to say, that knowing as you do, that the worst thing of all is to regret the things you should have done...but you're still hesitating, then allow us remind you of the speeding clock.

Tick Tock

Time speaks softly but carries a big stick.

PART 5

THE ART OF
DECISION-MAKING

"Indecision becomes decision with time."

Anon

"You've got a lot of choices. If getting out of bed in the morning is a chore and you're not smiling on a regular basis, try another choice."

Steven D. Woodhull

There's a natural order of things. It goes like this:

Decide —————————————➤ **Then act.**

Doing comes after a decision. And like it or not you are about to make a decision.

With every force of reason and emotion and the joy of life you are about to decide to scratch your damn itch.

But if you choose to put off making a decision you are still making a decision. By making no decision, you are making a decision. And by default the path you choose is not to change things.

Not being decisive on this matter means you are choosing to stand outside the ropes and be a bystander of your own life.

The decision-making muscle

The decision-making muscle is like any other, the more decisions you make, the stronger and better it gets. Sure it may seem easier to sit on the fence and "hope" things will change. They might, then again, they might get worse.

But if you are flexing your decision-making muscle, analyzing your options, thinking creatively about the way forward then you are in the driving seat. And even if (or let's face it, when) you occasionally make the wrong decision, you'll achieve far more than those who don't.

Make a decision. Then act on it.

Voilà! You have propulsion.

"When you have to make a choice and don't make it, that is in itself a choice."

William James

The seduction of research

Contemplation. Research. Analysis. Consideration. Evaluation...
Paralysis.

Aren't there just a million wonderful ways to put off making a
decision?

This danger of "drift" has been around since Stone Age man invented
navel-gazing but, as we said in Part 1, the Internet has multiplied these
possibilities endlessly. That's what makes action more urgent now
than ever before.

There's such volume and mass of information and opinion at our
fingertips that hundreds of millions of us are hooked on the idle
"activity" of finding out more information; on seeking ever more
fascinating and entertaining "research".

The author Nicholas Carr, who wrote *The Shallows: What The Internet
is Doing To Our Brains*, warned that tools like email caused people
to become addicted to **"mindlessly pressing levers in the hope of
receiving a pellet of social or intellectual nourishment"**.[16]

It's fun but it gets you nowhere. Fast.

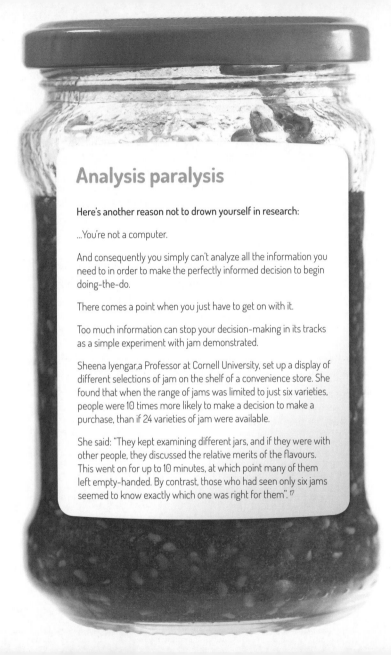

Analysis paralysis

Here's another reason not to drown yourself in research:

...You're not a computer.

And consequently you simply can't analyze all the information you need to in order to make the perfectly informed decision to begin doing-the-do.

There comes a point when you just have to get on with it.

Too much information can stop your decision-making in its tracks as a simple experiment with jam demonstrated.

Sheena Iyengar, a Professor at Cornell University, set up a display of different selections of jam on the shelf of a convenience store. She found that when the range of jams was limited to just six varieties, people were 10 times more likely to make a decision to make a purchase, than if 24 varieties of jam were available.

She said: "They kept examining different jars, and if they were with other people, they discussed the relative merits of the flavours. This went on for up to 10 minutes, at which point many of them left empty-handed. By contrast, those who had seen only six jams seemed to know exactly which one was right for them". [17]

Deep Blue was the brain child of IBM boffins who wanted to develop a computer that could beat the best chess players in the world. To do this Deep Blue was built to win through sheer brute computing power: it could evaluate 200 million positions per second. It played against the reigning champion in 1997, Garry Kasparov. And controversially the computer won, with Kasparov claiming that he saw deep intelligence and creativity in the play of Deep Blue which suggested to him that there had been human intervention during the games.

This was denied by IBM and is still shrouded in controversy. In any event, you aren't a computer and you can't analyze 200 million positions per second.

So don't bother trying. But then again a computer never gets to build a spaghetti tower with a marshmallow on top. And if it ever gets an itch it can't scratch it.

Only you can decide to do that.

Now.

How losing yourself in the flow can help your decision-making

Wealth, as President Richard Nixon warned in a previous quotation, will not necessarily make you happy.

And you may recall that Abraham Maslow with his "Hierarchy of Human Needs" said what makes you happy is fulfilling your potential through the act of doing something with purpose or personal meaning.

In other words:

Doing + Meaning = Happiness

But we can develop this idea of how Doing makes you Happy even further. And this may help you ensure you are going to make the right decisions.

Because it turns out that the state of "doing" that makes you happiest is the one when you don't even think about the fact you are "doing".

By studying people who love doing what they do, the psychologist Mihaly Csikszentmihalyi[18] found that time really flies when you are so absorbed in an activity that you lose yourself. Singers, actors, athletes and painters (and no doubt window cleaners also) describe this as being "in the zone".

Csikszentmihalyi calls this state of being: *Flow*.

FLOW is a state you can only reach through doing something challenging. When you come upon this happy state you are so absorbed in what you are doing that actually you do not even notice the passage of time, how tired you are or even if you're hungry.

You can't notice these things because you are totally focused on using your skills and experience to accomplish whatever it is you are "doing".

Your grey cells are simply too busy to notice it's dinner time!

And the reason for that is because what you are doing is above averagely challenging.

The addition to the mix, then, is that the activity is challenging (but not too challenging) and demands you to develop a skill or ability in whatever it is you do.

So now we can revise our formula to this:

Doing + Meaning + Skill = Flow

Your nervous system can process 110 bits of information per second, says Csikszentmihalyi.

Listening and concentrating on what someone is saying takes about 60 bits per second. If your activity is so challenging and fulfilling that it is demanding upwards of 80 bits per second then you have increasingly less capacity to process messages from your body like: I need the toilet and you may fail to notice you are sitting in a funny position and your leg has just gone numb! Next time your leg goes numb and you fall over when you try to stand up it may just be that you have found your state of flow.

The Flow

You are in flow when you are engaged in the "optimal challenge". This means you are using higher than average skills to do something which is more difficult than average.

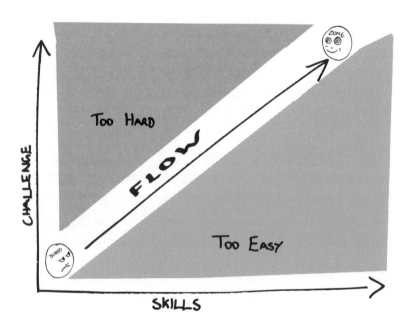

In his research Mihaly Csikszentmihalyi finds that flow is experienced by 15–20% of people every day while 15% of people say they never experience it.

In the state of flow you experience:
1. Total absorption in the activity
2. Loss of time awareness
3. Loss of self-awareness

The sort of activity that provides this feeling has these components:

1. Clear goals

2. Matches above average challenges with above average skills

3. Provides instant feedback as you go so that you know whether you are performing well or need to make adjustments

4. Personal control – you have a direct influence on the outcome of the activity

5. A high degree of concentration is required

As you make decisions about what you are setting out to do and how – check that it meets these criteria.

> "It does not seem to be true that work necessarily needs to be unpleasant.
>
> It may always have to be hard, or at least harder than doing nothing at all.
>
> But there is ample evidence that work can be enjoyable, and that indeed, it is often the most enjoyable part of life."
>
> Mihaly Csikszentmihalyi
> *Flow: The Psychology of Optimal Experience*

What you ought to know about the surprising lives of maximizers and satisficers...

One of the many ways psychologists define and segment people is by whether they want "only the best" (in which case they are maximizers) or whether they will settle for "good enough" (in which case they are satisficers).

As you consider your next step it might be helpful to know that satisficers tend to be happier with their decision-making than maximizers...even though maximizers do "better".

Take for example someone who gets back from work, falls back into their sofa and starts surfing TV channels to find something to watch.

A maximizer will surf through hundreds of channels – everything available – in order to find the definitive "best" channel to watch.

Meanwhile a satisficer will look for the first programme that is "good enough".

By the time the maximizer has found the "best" programme it is probably finished or it is 2am and it's time to hit the sack.

Their only comfort is that they were pretty sure what the best programme would have been...oh, if only they had watched it.

> "It has been said that man is a rational animal. All my life I have been searching for evidence which could support this."
>
> Bertrand Russell

Meanwhile a satisficer will watch the whole "good enough" programme and go to bed happy that they watched something pleasurable.

This might be ringing bells. Maybe you know people with a maximizing tendency. Perhaps you recognize it in the behaviour of friends who are seeking a romantic match, or even something as trivial as someone squeezing every single avocado at the grocer's.

But what does this mean when you transfer this maximizing/sufficing tendency from the idle world of TV watching to making the most important decisions in your life – like choosing and developing a career...

The impossibility of choosing the perfect job

Sheena Iyengar[19] (who carried out the jam experiment referred to earlier) and psychologists, Rachael Wells and Barry Schwartz investigated how maximizers and satisficers got on with job hunting when they graduated from college and how they felt about their subsequent careers. They found that:

During the process of researching jobs maximizers **applied for more jobs than satisficers**.

When they had received job offers maximizers **fantasized about jobs they were not even pursuing**.

And once they had accepted a job maximizers **wished they had pursued more options**.

They also found that maximizers had starting **salaries which were 20% higher** than satisficers.

But despite doing better financially, they felt worse about their situation and felt more "pessimistic, stressed, tired, anxious, worried, overwhelmed and depressed".

The scientists conclude that the search for the "best" solution is a route to guaranteed disappointment. The best solution is always elusive. As many of us know – the grass is always greener in your head than the grass you are standing on!

In other words you need to marry your ambition with pragmatism. Make a decision that you can stick with and then throw yourself behind that decision.

As the brilliant mathematician, philosopher, libertarian, campaigner for women's rights and the controversial founder of the Campaign for Nuclear Disarmament Bertrand Russell said – in typically precise language:

"When a difficult or worrying decision has to be reached, as soon as all the data are available, give the matter your best thought and make your decision; having made the decision, do not revise it unless some new fact comes to your knowledge. Nothing is so exhausting as indecision, and nothing is so futile."

Are you a Maximizer or Saticficer?

Give yourself points out of 5, where 5 is "Strongly like me" and 1 is "Not like me at all"

1. I like my job but I'm always on the lookout for something better. ☐

2. At a restaurant, I find it hard to choose what to eat. I don't want to regret it and wish I had what someone else ordered. ☐

3. If I have a special occasion to attend, I will devote a lot of time to finding exactly the right thing to wear. ☐

4. When I'm watching TV, I often flick through other channels just to see if there's something better on. ☐

5. I often cancel a social engagement if something else comes up that I think will be more interesting or fun. ☐

6. I spend a lot of time and effort trying to get exactly the right gifts for friends and family. ☐

7. In the past, I've turned down places (flat, house etc) to live because they don't fit with my idea of my ideal home.

8. I do a lot of research about holiday destinations before making a booking.

9. When I receive a gift token, I take a long time deciding what to spend it on.

10. When planning a journey, I make sure I've thought about all possible ways of getting there.

Between 30 – 50 points:

You're most probably a "Maximizer". You like to take your time and weigh a wide range of options — sometimes every possible one — before taking action.

Between 10 and 30 points

You're more likely a "Satisficer" (the word "satisfice" blends "satisfy" and "suffice") You would rather be fast than thorough; you prefer to simply choose the option that fills the minimum criteria and get on with it.

PART 6

...AND ACTION

"Wait!"

Winnie the Pooh

"How do you eat an elephant? One bite at a time."

A well-used saying

Here

This is the calm before the storm.

Just before rampaging into the world of doing – pause and take a breath – because a little bit of planning is called for right now.

And, once equipped with a cunning plan, it will pay dividends to investigate just which actions and habits will help you actualize the plan and which of them are just holding you back.

A bit of planning

Willpower alone will not get you to wherever you want to be.

You need a plan. Without planning the ascent on your personal Mount Everest your chances of success are little better than they are of winning the lottery.

Making the right plan starts with defining the right goals.

What's your goal?

But wait, you may be thinking, we've covered this already, surely?

The goal is the itch?

Well, yes and no.

Setting a goal for the plan is about setting a goal that is reasonable and achievable. In other words it has to be practical. Your itch might be to be a world famous climber, to run your own business, to travel the world, to make art. But to make this a reality we need to get down to measurable specifics – to set up an organic farm shop in nine months' time; to purchase a round-the-world ticket by Christmas; to put on a summer show of your best 10 paintings.

Keep it Real

The problem with fantasy goals

Keep a wary eye out for inappropriate goals. One trap that talkers fall into is to deliberately set a goal that is either impossible or such a long shot that it just about guarantees failure.

Which raises the question: Why would they do that?

Well, it turns out that the people who choose such fantasy goals are those who are most paralyzed by the fear of failure.

And the reason they choose goals that are self-evidently doomed to fail is that they pre-empt the fear of failure. The failure is already accepted. In this way, what they do by announcing they are pursuing a goal that neither they nor anyone else believes they will achieve, is to liberate themselves from failing.

Alas, the goal then lives in the world of fantasy and the talker is never held to account by real life.

In fact they are freed from the burden of really starting.

The **SMART** way to set goals was developed by the writer Paul J. Meyer[20]. This provides a framework to set a goal that you can achieve.

It is described by another writer, Robert Kelsey,[21] like this:

Specific (not "lose weight" but "lose 10 pounds")
Measurable ("lose 10 pounds by June")
Achievable (i.e. within the bounds of possibility – travel to Mars, for instance, may be a few generations hence)
Realistic (maybe a half marathon is more realistic this year, with a full marathon next year)
Timed ("June" it is)

Setting a real, achievable, measurable goal is then critical:

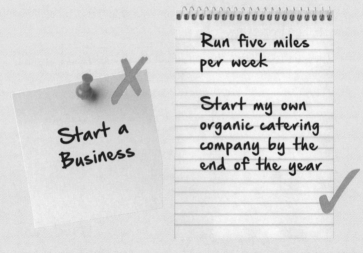

This won't work   This will

Goalodicy

Measure your goal for any symptoms of goalodicy ("the pursuit of idiotic goals").

If you suffer from goalodicy then you will find yourself so obsessed by the future goal that you ignore the practical realities of your situation. In fact you will think that in some magical way the achievement of the goal in the future will save you from all the difficult work, sacrifices and choices you really need to make along the way.

This suspension of reality leads to reckless behaviour; you can become so obsessed by the goal that you take unethical financial risks, dangerous personal risks or even, say, put at risk the security of your family.

In other words you are hereby warned to keep your feet planted on the ground at the same time as your ambition soars.

The phenomenon of goalodicy was described by D. Christopher Kayes[22] who studied the disastrous 1996 Everest Expedition in which amateur climbers paid huge sums to professional climbers to take them to the summit of the world's highest mountain.

As the conditions of the climb changed the climbers ignored their experience and expertise, says Kayes, because of their single-minded focus on reaching the summit. Normally they would have taken a different course of action and retreated.

But in their determination to reach the summit they ignored their realities and the expedition culminated in eight deaths and many life-long and disfiguring injuries for other survivors.

Kayes's six characteristics of goalodicy are well summed up by Kelsey:

- A narrowly defined goal (to get to the summit)

- Public expectation (these were ambitious people – including a celebrity writer – concerned about how they were perceived both within and beyond the group)

- Face-saving behaviour (from both the climbers and the leaders who might have ignored danger signals in order to maintain their credibility)

- A dream of an idealized future (of conquering Everest)

- Goal-driven justification (if the goal becomes "everything" it can be used to justify irrational decisions that may be dangerous)

- A sense of destiny

Is this ringing any bells?

"A dream is your creative vision for your life in the future. A goal is what specifically you intend to make happen.

Dreams and goals should be just out of your present reach but not out of sight. Dreams and goals are coming attractions in your life."

Joseph Campbell

Planning

Having successfully defined the goal we need a plan.
The plan will:
i) break down the journey into bite-size achievable parts and
ii) provide a critical path.

Chunk it down

This is critical. Viewed in its entirety the journey from talking to doing can appear so overwhelming that it is paralyzing.

By examining the constituent parts of the whole the project becomes less intimidating; it allows you to focus your energy on the right elements and to do it in the right order.

For example losing 2 pounds a month sounds far more focused than losing 2 stone in a year. It allows you to measure your progress, reward your progress and react to changes as your plan bumps into real life.

And you can be sure that whatever your plan is it will be sorely tested as soon as it faces the intervention of real life.

As the impressively named 19th-century Field Marshal Helmuth von Moltke the Elder of the Prussian Army said:

> "No plan survives contact with the enemy."

This isn't to say that there's no point having a plan but that your plan may have to be adapted from time to time once you start implementing it.

"The older I get the more wisdom I find in the ancient rule of taking first things first. A process which often reduces the most complex human problem to a manageable proportion."

Dwight D. Eisenhower

Chunk it Down Right Now

Chunking is a way of breaking down larger goals into more realistically achievable steps. By creating a series of realistic mini goals to achieve, you can also feel a continual sense of achievement, which in turn, will spur you on further.

Here's what to do:

1. Write down what, specifically, your goal is. For example, your goal might be "To open a barber's".

2. Break this goal into key steps you would need to take to achieve your goal. In this case:

   - Arrange finance
   - Find suitable premises
   - Fit out the premises with equipment
   - Employ staff
   - Advertising and Marketing

3. Next, break down these goals into smaller goals and tasks. Write down all you can think you will need to do to achieve these tasks / goals. No need to think about what order you will do these tasks, just write them all down.

4. With each of these smaller goals, break them down into even smaller tasks and goals. Each time you do this you are creating manageable tasks.

It may help to create a visual map of your goal.

1. Start by drawing a small circle in the middle of a sheet of paper and inside it write your goal. For example, "To open a barber's".

2. Next, draw circles for the key steps you'll need to take to achieve the main goal; in this case; Finance Premises, Equipment, Staff, Marketing.

3. Then draw lines (spokes) out from each of these circles and write everything you think you need to do to achieve that goal.

The real power of chunking is in the small, achievable steps. They allow you to focus on what you can achieve without feeling overwhelmed. Keep your eyes firmly on the next step and work steadily towards that. In good time, you'll be looking back in amazement at how far you have come!

Get that piece of paper right now and start writing!

The Critical Path

This is a project management term used in business to describe the sequence of events that a team must follow in order to deliver a goal in a certain time. If one event is delayed by a day, the whole project will be delayed by a day.

For our purposes the critical path simply means you need to work out in what order your chunks of work have to be completed to get the result you want.

First Things First

Create your critical path

You'll have identified all the smaller tasks, activities and goals in the previous "Chunk it down now" activity. Now you can create a "critical path".

Here's how:

1. Estimate how long each step will take. What's the least and most amount of time that each step might take?

2. Which activities are "critical", meaning that they have to be done on time or else the whole project will take longer? For example, with the barbers, the plumbing has to be installed in the time allotted for it otherwise it will delay all other activities.

3. Which steps are dependent on other steps being completed first?

   For example, with the barbers, the fixtures and fittings can't be installed until the premises are decorated but decoration can't take place till the plumbing is completed. So, the plumbing is "critical". If it's delayed for a day, a week, a month etc it will delay achievement of the whole project for – a day, week etc.

4. Which steps and tasks can be delayed, if necessary, without seriously delaying achievement of the main goal?

5. Which steps are not dependent on other steps happening first; can be taken at any time or at the same time as other steps?

6. Now write out all the steps that need to happen for another task to begin. Add in all the other steps where appropriate.

You now have a logical list and plan to guide you.

So what does an actual critical path look like? Well, let's take setting up a business as an example. What are the steps that you would need to take and in what order to give yourself the greatest chance of success? One thing's for sure, don't jump ship until you have a "critical path" in place!

Let's say you want to open up an organic cafe, but you're currently working in, say, HR. Your "critical path" would begin with research and planning – all of which will be done in your "spare time" and here's what that path might look like:

Path to a successful organic cafe

Location: where are you going to open up this organic cafe? A city centre will be a lot more expensive than by the coast. So is this part of a whole life change or just a business one?

Cost: how much is it going to cost you? Are you leasing or buying the premises? How many staff will you need? Will you need to invest in equipment or furniture? How much stock will you need to buy? How much are you going to charge for your food? What profit margins will you need to make a profit? Etc. etc.

Business plan: once you have a good idea of costs, you can start on a business plan. Without one would be like crossing the seas without a compass. Not a very clever idea.

Raise money: now you've decided on a location, have figured out how much it will all cost you, how to make a profit and how much cash reserves you need to get there…you need to figure out where you are going to get that cash from. You might choose to use your savings or draw down equity from your home. You may downsize or take out a loan. You may even do a combination of all the above.

Jump: once you've got your finance in place, you're ready to ...jump!

What if you're not starting a business?

Well, the same rules apply whether you are relocating to the coast, changing careers, running a marathon or losing a dress size.

Simply put, you need to know the steps you need to take and in what order to take them in order to get there.

Once you've got that, your chances of success increase exponentially.

Things to help you on your journey and things to trash

Now that you are moving deep into the land of doing you should use every tool you can to ensure you stick to the course... and be careful not to rely on thoughts and activities which use up energy and do not help.

Fortunately we can benefit from the study of 5000 people worldwide by Richard Wiseman, Britain's only Professor for the Public Understanding of Psychology.

The author of the highly recommended book, *59 Seconds*[23], found five steps that help maintain motivation throughout the course of a project...and five that don't...

Five actions that help

All these actions will have a psychological benefit and are proven to help you scratch your itch.

✓ 1. Public commitment

Tell people close to you, friends, family, work colleagues, about your plan and commit to them that you will see it through.Human beings are far more likely to see a project through if they have made their ambition public. And of course you'll only get support in the difficult times from people who know about the battle you are waging.

DO IT NOW: Talking about your plan is a good way to see who is on your side and who might hold you back. Don't just talk about your plan to everyone and their dog; choose the right people to tell.

Write down the names of the positive people in your life who you can talk to about your plan and who will support you.

Someone who has achieved what I want to achieve

_____

Someone who will give me ideas and advice

_____

Someone who will support me with setbacks

_____

Someone who will tell me how well I'm doing

_____

Someone who isn't afraid to challenge what I'm doing; who will make me stop and think about each step

---

Someone who's fun and will celebrate milestones with me....

The people on your list could be family, friends or colleagues. They might be professional advisors. Whoever they are, search them out and tell them what you're doing.

✓ **2. Step by step**

Chunk the work into pieces as discussed. By making the work manageable and bite-sized you reduce the chances of being over-awed and increase the opportunities for microsuccesses along the way.

DO IT NOW: See exercise on page 186

✓ **3. Rewards along the critical path**

And as you achieve each success along the way – celebrate!
Have a sweet (unless weight loss is your itch!); buy flowers; play some music; have a night off. Whatever seems appropriate.

DO IT NOW: Write down the things you enjoy doing. Then, when you reach a milestone on your critical path choose a reward.

✓ 4. Writing a record

Marking your progress in a physical way helps. Writing a diary, drawing charts of your journey, drawing pictures...all these things help make the process real; remind you of what you have achieved and keeps you focused on the next step.

> DO IT NOW: There are several ways you can do this:
>
> - Keep a diary
> - Take photos of each task as it is completed, each goal that is achieved
> - Draw pictures
> - Create a chart or graph to record progress

✓ 5. Do it for the right reasons

Reminding yourself of the positive reasons why you are working hard towards your goal will help keep you on course. Whether it is the clothes you can wear having lost weight or the decisions you will make once you become your own boss – thinking about this helps.

> DO IT NOW: To help remind yourself, write down your reasons from page 31 and put that piece of paper somewhere you'll regularly see; on the fridge, on your desk, on your phone as a screensaver.
>
> Or have an image – a picture or photo of what success will look like.

Five actions that *don't* help

These actions are neutral. At best. Since they don't help; don't waste your energy on them.

✗ 1. Motivating yourself by hero-worshipping someone

As Wiseman wrote in *59 Seconds* about the participants in his research: "[People who put] a picture of Elle Macpherson or Richard Branson on their fridge door did not tend to drop that all-important clothing size or achieve their business ambitions."

✗ 2. Doing it for the wrong reasons – thinking about failure or how you hate what you're doing

Trying to motivate yourself by thinking about how miserable you are because of the unscratched itch, or how terrible you will feel if you fail, will not work. Negative thinking such as this will not help you focus your energy and discipline on the goals you have set.

Goals that contain "don't", "mustn't" or "stop" are self-defeating. Instead of thinking, for example, "I hate this job. I can't work here any longer, I've got to stop" think "I am going to get a job doing work I enjoy and working with people I like."

Positive goals tell you what to do rather than what not to do. You are more likely to achieve goals that get you what you want, rather than goals that help you to avoid something.

Goals that are framed in such terms as "mustn't", "can't", "won't" or "shouldn't" do not serve to motivate you! To increase your chances for achieving any goal, think of a positive goal with a positive outcome.

Go back to your reasons for doing what you want to do. Are you sure they are framed in positive terms? If not, rewrite them.

✗ 3. Suppressing unhelpful thoughts

You can't diet by refusing to think about cream cakes. The more energy you put into not thinking about something the more energy you send in that direction. Don't think about a pink elephant for 10 minutes...got it?

Take a mindful approach: With mindfulness, rather than suppress an unhelpful thought, you acknowledge it, accept it then let it go and then turn to more helpful thoughts.

For example, you might say to yourself, "Here's a thought about a cream cake" Or "Here's a thought that I might fail as a freelancer." Or " Here's a thought that I won't complete the marathon race."

Having **acknowledged** the unhelpful thought, you can let it go. Then you focus on positive, helpful thoughts about what you can do rather than what you can't have or do. You turn your attention to what positive, helpful things you can do.

For example, "Here's the thought that I won't complete the marathon race." Once you've acknowledged that thought you think of something more positive and helpful. "I could fit in one more training run each week and ask a running friend to come with me for support."

✗ 4. Fantasizing about scratching the itch

Those who daydream about how fabulous life will be once they achieve their goal are less likely to get there. Because they are focused on having achieved success and not about the process of getting to success they are unprepared for bumps and hiccups along the way. They are probably also more likely to be disappointed by the distance between where they are today and where they want to be. The lesson is that while it's nice to fantasize about the goal – it won't get you there!

So instead of daydreaming, talk to yourself - making use of your inner talk is one of the most effective ways to master your mind and foster success.

Research[24] shows that if you address yourself by your name your chances of doing well with a host of tasks, can soar. It can focus your thinking and planning.

How come? Well, for many of us, it's easy to advise and encourage a friend yet when it comes to ourselves, we're not so good. It turns out that rather than telling yourself for example, "This is what I'm going to do next" if you address yourself using your name ("Amy, this is what you're going to do next") you are distancing yourself from your self and that helps you take action.

It would appear that this psychological distance encourages self-control, allowing you to think clearly, and perform more competently.

Try it!

✗ 5. Relying on willpower alone
Willpower isn't a plan and isn't a support structure. It's important but it doesn't get you the whole way there and trusting it alone will lead to disappointment.

If the smallest task still seems too hard, say you're just going to do 5 minutes of that small task right now. Or just two minutes. Make it ridiculously easy.

Tell yourself, "This is what I'm going to do next" and have just one thing you can do right now. Instead of saying you're going to do it at some point, say "I'm going to do it right now".

[Source: 59 Seconds, Professor Richard Wiseman, PanMacmillan, 2009]

The futility of using willpower alone as a way to achieve even a short-term goal was demonstrated once again by psychologists in possession of marshmallows!

The researchers told a group of four-year-old children, in individual tests, that they would receive extra marshmallows if they could restrain themselves from eating a single marshmallow left on a table when the researcher left them alone in a room for up to 20 minutes. The kids who stared grimfaced and determined at the marshmallow and tried to get through this time period through sheer willpower failed.

Those who made it focused their energy on HOW they would get through the period – they sang songs, covered their eyes or walked around the room. Many years later researchers tracked down the kids – by then adolescents. Those who had lasted the 20-minute trial and demonstrated their ability to "delay gratification" and control their impulses had achieved happier lives as measured by being psychologically better adjusted and scoring significantly higher in their US high school Scholastic Aptitude Tests.[25]

This won't work.

A personal slogan

Yes – listen up, cynics – you need one of these.

A slogan. A mantra. A device to help you get into the positive habits that will help propel you toward continued doing.

And it also serves as a thumping great mallet with which to bonk yourself on the head if you start slipping back into the noisy and directionless world of talking.

So choose a slogan. Make one up. Whatever works for you.

Let's say it's "TALK IS CHEAP" – stick it to your bathroom mirror, your desk lamp, your fridge – wherever you need it.

Or make it the wallpaper on your computer or your phone.

Walk the talk

A little less conversation, a little more action please

Actions speak louder than words

Regret weighs more than fear

"It's not bragging if you can back it up"

Be a contender

You gotta be in it to win it

I AM a contender

Time for action

Carpe diem: Seize the day

My word is my bond

Let's dance

...Tick tock

Now what?

Now you grab life by the collar, shake it, shape it and own it.

You know your itch. You have translated it into
an achievable and measurable goal.

You know yourself so you know whether you will
commit to making this change a reality.

You know you need a plan.

You know what will help you and what won't.

You know regret weighs more heavily than fear.

You know for certain that the clock is remorselessly ticking.

You know that the sting in life's tail is how fast it flies by while you're
working out what's important and what isn't.

...And now it's down to you.

As the Tibetan Lama said in the story on the second page:

"The point is that if you don't put the big rocks in first you'll never get them in at all. What are your priorities in life?"

Everyone has unique challenges. You have to face your own demons and deal with the challenges of your personal circumstances.

Maybe your best path is to wait tables at night, live with your parents, and save your money to go travelling or run your freelance graphic design business during the day.

Perhaps you're too old, too proud, too alienated, have kids, or live too far away for that. Then this is your reality and you need to make a plan that works with it.

Maybe you recognize that your itch is to express yourself making art of some kind. Then you might question whether you should keep your day job and find the comfort that you can in knowing that your sub-optimal job affords you the money and the energy to make art in the evenings.

The scenarios are as endless as grains of sand and they are almost as plentiful as the excuses people create for not making their dreams real.

If you are going to do it then by now you know it.

Start.

Accreditations

1. (pii) *The Art of Looking Sideways*, Alan Fletcher, Phaidon, 2001

2. (p13) *Tribes*, Seth Godin, Piatkus Books, 2008

3. (p26) *Drive*, Daniel H. Pink, Canon Gate, 2011

4. (p26) *Creating a World without Poverty – Social Business and the Future of Capitalism*, Muhammad Yunus, PublicAffairs, 2009

5. (p31) "How many people have ever lived on Earth", Carl Haub, Population Reference Bureau

6. (p45) "Think Tank: Ever felt like your job isn't what you were born to do? You're not alone", Daniel Pink, *The Sunday Telegraph*, 26 February 2011

7. (p47) *A Theory of Human Motivation*, Abraham Maslow, *Psychological Review*, 1943

8. (p72) *The Conquest of Happiness*, Bertrand Russell, George Allen & Unwin, 1930

9. (p97) *The Spotlight Effect in Social Judgement: An Egocentric Bias in Estimates of the Salience of One's Own Actions and Appearance*, Thomas Gilovich of Cornell University, Victoria Husted Medvec of Northwestern University and Kenneth Savitsky of Williams College

10. (p120) *"To Do or To Have? That is the Question"*, Leaf van Boven at University of Colorado at Boulder and Thomas Gilovich of Cornell University, *Journal of Personality and Social Psychology*, 2003

11. (p125) *The Case for Working With Your Hands*, Matthew Crawford, Penguin, 2010

12. (p134) *The Procrastination Equation*, Piers Steel, Prentice Hall, 2010

13. (p137) "On finished and unfinished tasks", Bluma Zeigarnik, in W.D. Ellis (Ed.), *A Sourcebook of Gestalt Psychology*, Humanities Press, 1938

14. (p139) The marshmallow challenge, www.marshmallowchallenge.com

15. (p142) *Obliquity*, John Kay, Profile Books, 2011

16. (p157) Nicholas Carr in an interview with *Esquire* magazine in 2010

17. (p158) "When choice is demotivating. Can one desire too much of a good thing?", Sheena S. Iyengar of Columbia University and Mark R. Lepper of Stanford University, *Journal of Personality and Social Psychology*, 79 (6), December 2000

18. (p161) *Flow: The Psychology of Optimal Experience*, Mihaly Csikszentmihalyi, HarperPerennial, 1991

19. (p168) "Doing Better but feeling worse: Looking for the 'Best' job undermines Satisfaction," Sheena S. Iyengar and Rachel E. Wells of Columbia University and Barry Schwartz of Swarthmore College, *Psychological Science*, 17 (2), 2006

20. (p180) *Attitude is Everything*, Paul J. Meyer, Meyer Resource Group, Inc, 2003

21. (p180) *What's Stopping You?*, Robert Kelsey, Capstone, 2011

22. (p181) *Destructive Goal Pursuit*, D. Christopher Kayes, Palgrave Macmillan, 2006

23. (p191) *59 Seconds*, Richard Wiseman, Pan Macmillan, 2009

24. (p197) "Self-talk as a regulatory mechanism: How you do it matters", Ethan Kross et al, *Journal of Personality and Social Psychology*, 106 (2), Feb 2014.

25. (p198) The Stanford Marshmallow experiment was created by Professor Walter Mischel at Stanford University

Illustrations and images

Pix Deserted rural road – © travellinglight/istockphoto.com

P1, 136, 148, 203 Emperor Scorpion – © John Bell/istockphoto.com

P4 Scorpion silhouette – © Thomas Seybold/istockphoto.com

P10, 16, 24, 28 Counting Hands – © Yunus Arakon/istockphoto.com

P32 'Young And Ali In 1976 World Heavyweight Title Fight' (2005 Getty Images/gettyimages.co.uk)

P35 Mosquito – © Henrik Larsson/istockphoto.com

P38 Mosquitoes silhouette – © David Szabo/istockphoto.com

P39, 180, 201 Yellow Sticky Note – © Uyen Le/istockphoto.com

P39, 180 Blank isolated notepad – © rusm/istockphoto.com

P51 Paint Can on white – © John Clines/istockphoto.com

P62 Cheering crowd – © Stephen Spraggon/istockphoto.com

P64 Human pyramid - teamwork – © Mlenny Photography/istockphoto.com

P74 Megaphone – © Alex Slobodkin/istockphoto.com

P79 Boy jumping off the cliff – Can Balcioglu/Shutterstock.com

P94 Stone slab – © italianestro/istockphoto.com

P97 Clothing, T-Shirt – © Jason Lugo/istockphoto.com

P104 Ladder – © Bertold Werkmann/istockphoto.com

P110 Eurofighter (Typhoon) jet – Sascha Hahn/Shutterstock.com

P113 Photograph of Yogi in Varanasi, India by Herbert Ponting, 1907, from Wikipedia.org

P116 Dachshund puppy digging in beach sand – Denis Babenko/Shutterstock.com

P122 'Ulysses and the Sirens' (1891) by John William Waterhouse (1849–1917), from Wikipedia.org

P124 Graffiti photographs by Richard Newton

P125 50's TV commercial – © james steidl/istockphoto.com

P127 Over-enthusiastic rooster crossing the start line photograph by Rita Deavoll. We found out that this had been taken by a lady from New Zealand whilst on holiday in the Cooke Islands. So we sent Rita an email explaining our odd request for permission to use the photo and she generously sent us the original photo with her blessing. It just shows how connected and supportive the world is once you start doing things!

P133 Procrastination – © esolla/istockphoto.com

P135 Waldorf Astoria Hotel – © 1988 by James G. Howes

P138 Marshmallows – Lori Sparkia/Shutterstock.com

P151 Box of assorted chocolates – Mpanch/Shutterstock.com

P158 A jar of raspberry jam isolated – © Yuri Shirokov/Shutterstock.com

P169 'Lord Bertrand Russell' (Gamma-Keystone via Getty Images/gettyimages.co.uk)

P199 Photograph of child staring forlornly at the marshmallow, supplied by his mum

P200-201 Set red stickers – © MilaLiu/Shutterstock.com

P200-201 realistic red stickers with peeling corners – © sovisdesign/Shutterstock.com

P200-201 Set Of Blank Stickers – © U.P.images_vector/Shutterstock.com

Illustrations supplied by Jonathan Marsh: pages v, viii, 15, 27, 70, 178, 205

Illustrations supplied by Curtis Allen (www.curtisallen.co.uk): pages 40, 53, 60, 77, 144, 145, 188

All others by Richard Newton: pages 17, 31, 46, 84, 147, 164, 173

A graduate of The London School of Economics, Sháá Wasmund's entrepreneurial career had an unusual start. At 22 she won a competition to interview Super Middleweight boxing champ Chris Eubank and ended up helping to promote his next fight to a sell-out 48,000 live crowd and an 18 million TV audience. Sháá remains an ardent boxing fan.

Shortly after she set up her own PR and marketing company and won the then relatively unknown vacuum cleaner company Dyson as one of her first clients. Working alongside Sir James Dyson helping to establish Dyson as a global brand taught Sháá more about business than any MBA. To this day, Sháá credits James as being one her biggest sources of inspiration.

Sháá's love affair with the Internet began after she became a founding director in Sir Bob Geldof's online travel company. A year later, Sháá raised substantial funds to launch **mykindaplace.com** an early social networking site. The company was later sold to BSkyB.

Sháá is an international bestselling author, prolific public speaker, digital native and passionate champion of small businesses. Amongst other accolades, Sháá has been voted by the *Institute of Directors* as one of the UK's Most Connected Women.

In 2009 Sháá launched **Smarta.com**, the UK's #1 Resource for Small Business. In 2011 Sháá launched 'Smarta Business Builder', a groundbreaking cloud-based toolkit for business.

In 2015, Sháá was presented with an MBE from the Queen for her 'services to business and enterprise' and published her second #1 bestseller *Do Less, Get More: How To Work Smart and Live Life Your Way*.

Sháá now runs business bootcamps, workshops and coaching programmes under her own brand, **shaa.com**. She has helped thousands of people monitize their passions and knowledge to build digital businesses they love.

She's a regular guest on Sky Sunrise, reviewing the papers with Eamonn Holmes and now speaks on stages across the world, most recently sharing stages with Gary Veynerchuck and E-Myth legend Michael Gerber.

Follow Sháá:

Twitter: @Shaawasmund

Facebook: facebook.com/shaawasmund

Acknowledgements

This book is for all the people that allow me to Stop Talking and Start Doing. No one can create anything truly great in isolation.

To my Nan – they broke the mould when they made you. You are truly irreplaceable.

To my Mum, thank you for teaching me to live without limitations.

They say friends are the family you choose for yourself and that is certainly true of mine: Brenda, Lisa, Troy, Kanya, Hulya, Chloe, Michelle, Kelly, Kym, Chris, Matt, Andrew, Oli, Ambrose, Larry, Tim, Greg, Howard – I wouldn't be who I am without all of you.

To Rich for his support, brilliant writing skills and friendship.

To Gill for taking the original concept and creating powerful exercises around it.

Most of all, this is for my beautiful son Jett and his gorgeous, smart and funny Dad, Steve. We miss you every minute of every day. Love you big as the universe. This book is for you.

In acknowledgement of Richard Newton's contribution to the original edition, *Stop Talking, Start Doing*

Richard Newton is an entrepreneur, consultant and writer. After spending almost ten years writing about business for *The Sunday Telegraph*, *The Mail on Sunday* and others, Richard decided to switch sides, walk the talk and run his own business. He co-founded a software company that supplies brand management solutions for many of the world's largest consumer brands.

He is now a co-founder, director, board adviser and/or mentor at a number of tech companies and start-ups including Screendragon, Call Trunk and Txt2Buy.

He runs the consultancy Newton Principals and writes about being creative in business, the importance of good language in business, and the urgency TO DO THINGS!'

He writes at **richard-newton.com** and can also be reached at @richnewton.

Acknowledgements

So many people have given me a helpful kick me in the pants that I've worn out holes in other people's shoes. In any event, there are far too many people to mention by name. But I saw this sign in a café the other day and I think it says all I need.

To everyone:

And if I missed anyone out see above.

Notes

Notes

Notes